INDIA'S EDUCATED WOMEN :
OPTIONS AND CONSTRAINTS

STUDIES IN SOCIOLOGY AND SOCIAL ANTHROPOLOGY

Editor
M. N. Srinivas

Associate Editor
A. M. Shah

Advisory Board
Scarlett Epstein, Owen M. Lynch, T. K. Oommen

Other Titles in the Series

Biplab Dasgupta (ed.), *Village Studies in the Third World*

A. L. Epstein (ed.), *The Craft of Social Anthropology*

Prasanta S. Majumdar and Ila Majumdar, *Rural Migrants in an Urban Setting*

Miriam Sharma, *The Politics of Inequality*

T. Scarlett Epstein, *Capitalism, Primitive and Modern*

M. N. Srinivas, *India: Social Structure*

INDIA'S EDUCATED WOMEN:
OPTIONS AND CONSTRAINTS

Rhoda Lois Blumberg
and
Leela Dwaraki

HINDUSTAN PUBLISHING CORPORATION (INDIA)
DELHI   1980

305.40954
B658i

Printed in India by
Hindustan Publishing Corporation Printing Press
36-U.A., Jawahar Nagar, Delhi 110007

For Leah

PREFACE

A Fulbright-Hayes research fellowship, in 1966-67, enabled us to do the initial research upon which this book is based. The American Institute of Indian Studies provided assistance for the follow-up study in 1977. We are indebted, also, to the Rutgers University Research Council, which generously supported the project with grants.

In 1966-67, the then chairperson of the Bangalore University Sociology Department, Sri V. Muddalinganna, helped in many ways—both intellectually and practically. Again in 1977, the senior author and the junior author (one of his former students) benefitted from his friendship and support. Continuity between the two studies was greatly aided by the fact that the principal members of the original research team jointly undertook the follow-up. *Indian Women in Transition: A Bangalore Case Study* reported on the initial research and was published in 1972 under the sole authorship of Rhoda Blumberg.* Leela Dwaraki is co-author of the revised work, since she played a much larger role in the second phase, participating in all aspects of the research process and continuing data collection after Blumberg had returned to the United States. Responsibility for the writing rests with the senior author.

Maggie Matthews and B. S. Ramamani provided competent assistance at various stages of the initial research, as did Melissa A. Banks and Martha L. Lee during preparation of this new work. Homaira Begum Alauden, whom we met in the course of a pretest, proved to be an enduring friend upon whom one could count for intellectual discourse and analysis. Homaira did all that she could to assist us in our work during the follow-up phase, as well.

In the Summer of 1977, the senior author returned to India, hoping to find out what she could about the lives of the women that had been interviewed a little more than a decade earlier. The "Emergency" period of Indira Gandhi had just come to a close and people could speak freely about it. These first hand accounts clarified notions acquired through other sources. But the immediate purposes of the visit were more con-

---

*Her works prior to 1979 were published under the name Rhoda Goldstein.

fined : to observe, in any way possible, changes that might have taken place in the role of women, to attempt to contact the 1966-67 respondents, and to meet with scholars and old friends. (A description of the follow-up methodology will be found in Chapter 1.)

Both in Delhi and Bangalore we were able to meet with a number of knowledgeable people and to obtain their views about the decade's changes. Notable among these were Promilla Kapur, Rama Mehta, and Ivy Khan. Dr. Bina Roy was particularly gracious in arranging such contacts, sharing her own ideas, and directing us to recent important literature. The American Institute of Indian Studies had helped to arrange an affiliation with the Institute for Social and Economic Change in Bangalore. There we had the privilege of meeting Professor M. N. Srinivas, who expressed interest in having the original work republished in India. Scarecrow Press of Metuchen, New Jersey, the publisher of *Indian Women in Transition,* encouraged the venture.

This book presents most of the original findings intact. They were based on personal interviews, a favoured tool of the present authors, as it is of the women sociologists in India who have written most extensively on modern urban women. Probably unique about *Indian Women in Transition* were two elements : its use of a scientifically selected sample of women graduates and postgraduates of a particular university in a particular year, and the extremely high rate of response—resulting in 97 successfully completed schedules out of a sample of 99. Eight members of this original sample were found to have left Bangalore and were reached through use of a mail questionnaire. Perhaps this was fortunate, for their careful answers revealed that such an instrument could be used successfully with highly educated Indian women. We did indeed use a mail questionnaire in the follow-up, resulting in a 31 per cent rate of response.

In revising the work, we have commented upon earlier forecasts and interpretations where relevant, using both published literature and our own more recent data. Many of the specific findings of the 1966-67 study are presented in the language of the original edition; we have attempted, however, to put them into a broader context.

In addition to those mentioned, we would like to thank the following persons : for the first phase, Bernard Goldstein provided excellent critical judgment and support. Leah (Mary) Goldstein, to whom this work is ix

dedicated, is the senior author's eldest daughter. At a young age she took on many of the errands and tasks of the household so that her mother could work. Similarly, Meyer and Helena Jo Goldstein knew that their mother was also a working scholar and were extremely cooperative. In the course of the follow-up research, two family members of the junior author were particularly helpful and supportive—her father, Sri H. Nagappa, and her husband, B. R. Dwaraki. We are grateful to them. Finally, it was a joy to both of us to once again share an exciting research experience.

Among those in the United States who provided most encouragement for the re-study and revision of the first book, Shanti Tangri and Alfred Pantzer stand out. Fortunately, it was another highly competent friend, Marion Hajdu, who took on the job of typing the manuscript.

Many of those whom we met in the course of the research cannot be named, but we thank them for their warm hospitality and willingness to share their thoughts and their ideas.

RHODA LOIS BLUMBERG
LEELA DWARAKI

CONTENTS

Preface ... vii

Tables ... xii

Chapter 1

Introduction: Educated Women in a Changing Society ... 1

Chapter 2

Social and Economic Characteristics of the Bangalore Samples ... 14

Chapter 3

Students in Saris: The Meaning of Education ... 37

Chapter 4

Tradition and Change in Views of Marriage ... 57

Chapter 5

Work: A New Value for Daughters of the Middle Class ... 85

Chapter 6

Finding a Suitable Job ... 113

Chapter 7

Conclusion ... 133

Appendix ... 144

Notes ... 152

Bibliography ... 163

Index ... 169

TABLES

1. General Characteristics of the Bangalore Sample   18
2. Father's Occupations   21
3. Class Identification by Family Income   22
4. Fathers and Mothers of Respondents by Educational Level   26
5. Income, Caste and Religion by Number of Respondents' Siblings   28
6. Single, Married and Separated Respondents by Household Type   32
7. Comparison of Household Types of Bangalore Samples   34
8. Educational Level of Respondents by Current Activities and Plans   39
9. Women by Present Educational Level as they View Role of Education in Finding a Mate   40
10. Percentage Distribution of Ever Married Persons According to Sex and Age, 1961 and 1971   43
11. Opinions of Educated Women as to How they are Expected to Contribute to Society   55
12. Opinions about a Woman's Happiness Without Marriage, by Education and Marital Status   66
13. Comparsion of the Effects of Education and Employment on Marital Chances   74
14. How Employment Helps in Finding a Partner   75
15. Dowry Practices by Employment Status of Women   78
16. Distribution of Respondents by Religion and Caste by Current Employment and Educational Activity   92
17. Distribution of Respondents by Educational Levels by Current Employment and Educational Activity   93
18. Percentage Distribution of Activities Desired by Respondents in the Next Two Years   98
19. Reported Attitudes of Family Members about Respondent's Working   102
20. Current Status of Respondents by Attitudes of Selected Family Members   104
21. Respondents' Views of Conditions under which Married Women or Mother may Work   110
22. Respondents' Occupations by Salary   116
23. Type of Job and Salary Earned by Respondent's Description of Own Job   127

CHAPTER 1

INTRODUCTION : EDUCATED WOMEN IN A CHANGING SOCIETY

Providing a scientific base for policy making

THE literature on women in developing countries is increasingly being enriched by the research of women scholars, some of whom are not native to the geographical area of their special interest. They identify as "insiders" based on gender rather than nationality, and no longer hesitate to make international comparisons. They find that, through comparative study, they are able to reveal the variability in conceptions of womanhood, in norms governing women's roles, and in the roles themselves. They can observe the effects of political and economic development on women in different social and economic classes, in rural areas, towns and cities. From a historical perspective, they are able to note the forces affecting sex roles and sexual inequality and how these fluctuate in different epochs.

It is to this body of international literature that we hope to contribute, as we analyze the changing set of options and constraints experienced by a sample of highly educated Indian women.

The burgeoning of research on women has enlarged our scientific knowledge about societies. This provides a concrete base for intellectual leaders hoping to help guide their nations in the development process. A prime example of the use of research for policy purposes is the report of the Committee on the Status of Women in India, *Towards Equality* (Government of India, 1974). The report, issued after the publication of our first book, drew upon original studies and recent literature. It reflects the concern of India and other developing nations for uplifting the masses of their women.

Male dominance and female roles

In most societies of the world, women have been defined largely in terms of their functions as wives and mothers, and by cultural images of their sexuality. The rights of women to become educated and to hold jobs outside of the home have frequently been questioned; women who have *had* to work have tended to be of low economic and social status. Much of the early thrust of the American women's movement of the 1970's was directed toward the right of married women to be employed outside of the home and to be freed from total preoccupation with child care. Feminists tried to shatter long-held notions about "women's place" and the accepted myths about their nature and function. Women whose economic status left them no choice but to work were still faced with the dual burden of employment and household duties. And, at the beginning of the last decade, American women noted that, despite seeming progress, they still occupied positions inferior to men in every area of life—and that economic rewards, power and status were distributed inequitably to them. The recession of the middle seventies even led to a decline in some of the economic gains that they were able to attain through struggle in the early seventies (Steffes, 1975). Despite official ideologies of equality, males remained dominant economically, politically and socially.

The questioning by Western feminists of the naturalness of this male dominance is sometimes criticized by those who wish to avoid conflict. The attempts of women to raise the level of their own consciousness about themselves and their roles involves thinking through and confronting a number of paradoxes and choices. At first glance it seems unlikely that women should accept, and be happy in, inferior positions—yet this is frequently the case. One is forced to examine the gains to be found in unquestioning acceptance of male dominance. Here the experience of every situation of superordination-subordination is instructive. The "good" inferior, who plays out his or her role deferentially, earns the goodwill of the benevolent master. Treated as childlike, inferior, or helpless, he or she is the object of *noblesse-oblige*. Through artful manipulation, the inferior is able to get the most out of the system, whatever system it may be. The very servility or humility with which he or she approaches the master may be skillful pretense. And thus, in a way, the individual who does not have formal power achieves functional or informal power. The best exploration of this interrelationship, in the case of the female-male relationship, is to be found in Elizabeth Janeway's *Man's World, Women's Place* (1971 : 56). She sums up the point in this way :

 ... when women cling to their traditional role, it is not primarily because they find masochistic pleasure in being dominated (though no doubt some do) but because this role offers them power too : private power in return for public submission. This is the regular, orthodox bargain by which men run the world and allow women to rule in their own place.

Janeway's ideas are relevant to the present study. The formally subordinate role of Indian women to Indian men is spelled out in sacred literature, in law, and in practice. Yet there is no doubt that the woman who accepts this role and plays it out to perfection, the ideal Indian wife and mother, is revered and loved. Less happy is the situation of a woman who has been widowed, divorced, or remained single. She does not achieve this ideal but rather tends to remain a peripheral person in any household.

There is no doubt that many or most Indian women *do accept* their traditional role of dependence on male relatives. But as the possibility of economic independence, through respectable employment, becomes a reality for middle class Indian women, they may be allowed new options. If paid employment is the liberating factor that so many American feminists claim, is it so in every society and in every context ? Or are other elements needed?

The economic, political and social changes that combine together to create innovations need to be placed in their cultural context. That such changes have occurred in the lives of a number of urban middle class Indian women is not doubted.[1] The reformist movements of the last two centuries, the current needs and aspirations of middle class families, and the new opportunities for female education and employment, all interact to foster change. Similarly, technological innovation affects the lives of rural Indian women, sometimes in ways that are not favorable. Tradition, religious beliefs, and superstition retain important influence and, under changed conditions, may be transmuted into new forms.

Interaction of forces of tradition and modernity

How are new roles engendered by college education made to mesh with the traditionally family-centered female roles ? This book focuses on Indian women in transition, on the ways in which a group of young urban middle class women (and their families) deal with their expanded set of statuses. In what ways do Indian women expect to use their newly acquired higher education? How do they view its effect on their lives? What problems are encountered when, and if, they "take up jobs"? What kinds of jobs are available to them? As these questions are examined, we will be exploring ways in which the forces of tradition and modernity are or are not being reconciled. We will note whether higher education and entrance into employment modifies conceptions of women.

No one will deny the coexistence of the old and the new in India. The question is how they coexist : whether new practices create conflict and turmoil or are readily incorporated into traditional ones. Students of development have suggested that the potentialities for change lie within traditions (Gusfield, 1967; Rudolph and Rudolph, 1967). Gusfield (1967) writes of a "misplaced polarity" between tradition and modernity. Bondurant (1953) makes the case that the potential for change is an essential element in Hindu philosophy, as one of the aspects of *dharma*. And, indeed, India's vast body of religious and philosophical teachings has provided an ample source for social reformers who wished to validate twentieth century reforms by heralding back to ancient traditions more liberal than those inspired by foreign domination.

Thus, might it not be that the modern woman, impelled by traditional notions of sacrifice and duty, will work in order to contribute to her family, rather than to satisfy her individual aspirations? But what if the day-by-day requirements of an expanded set of roles then make it impossible for her to adequately fulfill traditional duties? What if the new role brings her into contact with beliefs and standards different from those she has known? What if it should make her susceptible to a "love" marriage, perhaps an inter-caste marriage? What if the ability to earn does create a more independent woman?

While the Western social scientist may be less aware of the uses of tradition to support new behavior patterns, he/she is unlikely to overlook the obvious potentialities for conflict. Given the unevenness of change, various role players will face inconsistent or conflicting expectations from others, and experience strain. Knowledge of such strains and contradictions in a given system provides clues about the possibilities of additional change.

The educated Indian woman, in contact with a broader culture than that of her home, learns about new role potentialities. The changes that college education bring about are varied; some women learn to live with inconsistencies while others are in more open conflict. The educated women that are studied vary in their willingness to verbalize feelings of conflict. A few whose notions of women's rights and roles differ from those of their elders are openly prepared to rebel; many find little discrepancy between their new roles and their loyalties to old ones, while others who languish privately continue to accede outwardly to the wishes of their elders, as Indian women have usually done.

Methodology in the first and follow-up study

The main research to be described took place in 1966-67 and will be referred to as "the 1967 study" or "the original study". The initial research aim was quite simple : to learn something about the roles of highly educated women in a changing society. The research site was Bangalore, a South Indian city of over one million inhabitants, which is the capital of Karnataka (then Mysore) State and the seat of Bangalore University.[2] A follow-up study was initiated in Summer, 1977, and completed in 1977-78. It will be discussed in more detail later in this chapter. The original study is described from the vantage point of the senior author.

During 1966-67, Sri V. Muddalinganna, chairman of the Sociology Department at Bangalore University, directed my attention to the increasing participation of women graduates in the work force. The employment of middle class women appeared to be a central consequence of the extension of higher education. It was decided to sample a group of graduates and post-graduates who had finished their work for a degree fairly recently. Questions were designed to get objective data about education, employment and family background as well as knowledge about how young women viewed the significance of education in their lives. (See the Appendix for the specific questions.)

A 20 per cent sample was taken of women who had graduated from Bangalore University in 1965, and who gave Bangalore home addresses, a universe of 483.[3] Ninety-nine women were selected for the sample, which included graduates with bachelor's, master's, medical and law degrees.[4]

Preliminary discussions with members of the Sociology Department and women M. A.'s in sociology chosen as research assistants led to the formulation of a questionnaire, which was pretested in September and October of 1966. The revised questionnaire was then administered personally by the research team, consisting of the author and three research assistants. Eighty-eight respondents, or 91 per cent of the total, were interviewed in this manner, usually at home but sometimes at the University or at work. Eleven women were not living in Bangalore at the time of the contact, and eight responded to a mail questionnaire. This phase of the work was completed in April 1967. However, an additional member of the sample was located in Chicago, Illinois and was subsequently interviewed by a female sociologist later in 1967. Thus, 97 cases are included, a 98 per cent response.

The decision to use a questionnaire was based on several considerations. Questionnaires are an accepted vehicle of social scientific inquiry in India. Suspicion could be (and was) allayed by a printed schedule bearing the official sponsorship of the Bangalore University Sociology Department. Members of the sample, having been educated in the English medium in college, were familiar with the language in its written form. The American author could be confident that her English, if difficult for some to understand, could be supplemented by the printed word. The instrument could be mailed to out-of-town respondents; mailed responses then provided a check on the clarity of wording.

There was little way of anticipating the extremely high rate of response. The cordiality with which interviewers were received in Indian homes was striking, when compared with what one has come to expect from over-surveyed groups. Families frequently acted as if the visit was an "auspicious" occasion. The presence of the foreign scholar assured an interview in the few cases where a first contact by assistants had been met with suspicion.[5] But while the opportunity to participate in the interviewing process provided a fascinating introduction to Indian life for the foreign sociologist, the same questions may be raised about my role as about that of any other foreigner doing such research. For this reason, the research procedure will be described in some detail. The noted sociologist M. N. Srinivas (1966) has pointed out that there are disadvantages as well as advantages to the study of a culture by those native to it. At the same time, the foreign field worker is enjoined to develop the necessary sensitivity to and empathy with the culture he or she is studying. Some of the research procedures which evolved were not typical of research done in the United States, but seemed suitable and natural in India. Among these were the practice of interviewing in teams of two, and of interviewing individuals in the presence of other family members.

Almost all of the interviews were administered by various combinations of two assistants, one a Brahmin and the other a Christian, and the senior author.[6] Another Brahmin helped in the initial stages. The three assistants had been part of the same educational world as the young women being interviewed. Assistants were selected who could speak several languages and who would be able to conduct interviews in the respondents' mother tongue. In most cases this proved unnecessary. Many were fluent in the language and used it in informal contacts with friends as well as in formal situations. This was especially true of Christian and Moslem respondents, not all of whom knew Kannada, the main language of Karnataka State. One assistant's fluency in Kannada and Tamil, and familiarity with Urdu, was especially helpful in finding our way about the city and in conversing with neighbors and older family members.

In the main, we adapted to the Indian convention that females should not travel about the city alone. However, the Christian assistant was less bound by this tradition, and did some interviews herself. In later stages, the author also did this. Such interviews were arranged when the respondent could be expected to be very fluent in English, and after success had been experienced by the author in the team interviews.

As Hanna Papanek (1964 : 160) points out, the foreign woman field worker "not only has access to local women but can occupy a surprisingly flexible position in local society." Besides being free to travel about alone without censure, the author could meet privately with Indian females. I was also regarded as somewhat distinct from other female "elders" because of my unique status. The assistants soon became accustomed to a democratic approach and told others, "She is like a friend."

When the other two assistants had left for permanent posts elsewhere, Leela, the project mainstay, continued to interview. Her practice then was to take along a sister or a friend for accompaniment; such assistance from female friends and relatives was not considered an imposition.

In working together, the author and assistants acted as a team, wordlessly deciding which of the partners was to administer the interview schedule. If the respondent was fluent in English and seemed interested in talking to the American, she was interviewed by the author. An assistant could and did conduct the interview if the subject had difficulty in understanding American English or preferred to speak in Kannada.[7] Twenty of the interviews were conducted wholly or mostly in Kannada; the remainder in English. This procedure was developed as we assessed the reception of the interview team.

An equal number of interviews were conducted in privacy as in the presence of one or more family members—almost 44 per cent of each. The remaining 13 per cent took place in the company of a friend of the respondent. The presence of sisters or girl friends during the interviews seemed to make the respondents more comfortable, gayer, and more informal. Given a culture in which young women are often accompanied by their friends, the group situation was a very natural one. In cases where a parent was present in the room, one member of the interview team was usually able to engage him or her in a separate conversation. Occasionally a young woman would fill out the questionnaire herself while we talked to the parents. This enabled her to express private views which might be at variance with those of family members. Despite the obvious disadvantages, the group situations made it possible for us to converse with more family members informally than would have occurred otherwise.

Assistants were instructed to write down their comments after leaving the interview situation. All quotations from interviews and additional conversations are reproduced in the original to provide an authentic and immediate flavor of the tone and style of the interviewers' impressions and the interviewee's responses. They seem, in many ways, to be attitudinally revealing. The remarks of assistants, which will be quoted from time to time, proved very instructive as examples of peer group judgment. For instance, the most extremely reticent respondent, who depended on her father for assistance throughout the interview, was described in the following way by an assistant :

> The girl has no individuality whatsoever. For everything she was depending on her father's reply . . . . She was very shy . . . . I was quite surprised to know that a graduate is unable to answer a simple question like at what age a girl should get married . . . The interview wasn't very impressive but it is interesting to know that there are such types of girls in spite of education [Research Assistant A, about interview 106].

An initial obstacle was that of locating the desired respondent. Addresses had to be culled from various University lists. The assistants were unfamiliar with many Bangalore neighborhoods, and street addresses had been changed twice during the previous few years. Starting our interviews in areas familiar to the assistants provided the needed confidence to explore more difficult locations. Much use was made of informal contacts to find women who had married or moved for other reasons. The Moslem respondent referred to later in a footnote was located through inquiries among neighbors in the vicinity of her parents' former home.

In almost all cases, locating an address resulted in the ultimate granting of an interview. If no one was at home, we left a card making an appointment for our return. The research assistants utilized the convention of selecting a time and date for our future appointment, in the expectation that the individual would try to be at home when we returned. Through knowledge of the working schedules of government offices and schools we could choose times appropriate for working respondents.[8]

Assured the hospitality of Indian homes, how could we judge the honesty of responses? Both objective and subjective observations helped. The home and style of life of a respondent could be noted, as well as her identification of the family's class position. Cultural conventions about the kinds of information one makes public were revealed in the ease and rapidity, or reticence, with which certain answers were given. Data about the education of family members tended to be presented with great specificity. Informants occasionally mentioned that age or family income had been represented differently for official purposes, such as gaining scholarships. Naming one's salary fairly accurately seemed to be standard procedure for members of the sample. The opinions of family members on various issues were expressed with little hesitation. However, questions which sought the young woman's own opinion did cause some difficulty. For example, a number of women professed that they had not thought about their own future marriages. In Chapter 4 an analysis is made of this particular response, which turned out to be the conventionally modest one. In some cases the conventional response was not given, leading us to formulate a hypothesis about the deviant cases.[9]

Many respondents volunteered information about the arranged marriage system and the fact that it was not appropriate for them to think about marriage. However, they were quite willing to discuss the marriages of friends or other family members. It was here that some respondents would talk about the anxiety of women (never themselves) to get married.

A range in willingness to express independent thinking was observed. Some women were highly articulate and philosophical; others gave brief answers and appeared to be reticent to state their individual opinions. Perhaps the most difficult thing for the researcher to ascertain, in such a situation, is whether the individual is following convention or truly has no independent opinion on the matter at hand. Margaret Cormack's assertion (1961) that the Hindu woman's strong identification with family inhibits her sense of individuality is evident in some cases.[10]

Rama Mehta (1970), in her study of 50 highly educated Indian women, suggests that there are areas in which Indian women accept the right of parents to make decisions for them.   She states, "They had been brought up to leave important decisions to their parents. They were not reared to take responsibility for their actions and the right of their parents to marry them was part of their whole upbringing" (1970 : 112).   However, a related aspect of her training makes the Indian women unwilling to express disagreement with her parents when she *does* have an independent opinion. Many answers also reflect a reliance on fate or a belief that fate will determine one's future. Thus, even when encouraged, some respondents appear to be unable or unwilling to look into the future.   They find it difficult to respond to a question which asks what they would like to do in the next few years if given free choice. Varying degrees of fatalism are also expressed in answers about marriage.

An indication of change is the fact that some respondents openly expressed disagreement with their parents.   In contrast to Cormack's generalization, new types of women are emerging who take a more active stance toward their fate and who assert individuality.

In July, 1977, a follow-up study of the original sample was initiated by the senior author and Leela Dwaraki (who had assisted in the original study).   Respondents were contacted at their addresses of ten years earlier, first by a return postcard and later by mailed questionnaires.   In the postcard we asked for new addresses and invited the women to contact us.

Basic data about marital status, number of children, household composition, employment, work history and salary were sought. Some questions were asked about the problems of educated women and changes that had been observed in the position of women over the last ten years.

We hypothesized that possible bias in returns might occur as a result of inability to reach women whose families had moved their places of residence. Those whose families were homeowners at the time of the original study were more likely to be at the same addresses. Follow-up contacts were made, and the authors visited some neighborhoods in an attempt to locate respondents. The mail contacts proved more successful, and many families provided forwarding addresses.

Thirty questionnaires, representing 31 per cent of the 1967 sample, were received.   In addition, we interviewed three of the women and visited the family of another who was living abroad. Eleven of the 25 married subjects who responded to the follow-up are no longer living in Bangalore, and two of them reside in other countries. We also received information that at least five women whom we were unable to contact directly are living outside of India. It is apparent that an unusual amount of geographic mobility has been experienced by these highly educated women.

Value and limitations of the longitudinal data

Comparing the 1977 sample with the original one, we find that the median age of those who answered is 32—just ten years older than the median age of those interviewed in 1967. The proportions of Hindus, Christians and Moslems who responded closely resemble those of the original sample, as will be seen in Chapter 2. Since the original identifying code numbers had been retained, we were able to check the relative family economic status of those included in the follow-up. In 1967, 60 per cent of sample members had family incomes in the range of between Rs 300 and Rs 799 per month. Of those answering in 1977, 55 per cent reported 1967 family incomes in this range. A somewhat higher proportion of those responding to the new study had 1967 family incomes of Rs 800 or more— 45 per cent as compared to 33 per cent of the total 1967 sample—thus bearing out our expectations. In Chapter 2 we shall deal with class identification in more detail. However, it can be noted that those answering the follow-up fall wholly within the vast majority of subjects who, in 1967, identified themselves as "middle-middle" or "upper-middle" class. Thus, although the follow up group includes a slightly disproportionate number of women with somewhat higher 1967 family incomes, it does closely resemble the original sample.

The only other follow-up study of Indian women with which we are familiar is one done by Promilla Kapur (1974), who administered the same questions to different but matched groups of women over a ten year interval. The sampling procedures used in our initial study, and the unusually high rate of return (98 per cent) suggest that our original findings accurately represent the situation of women graduates and post-graduates of the year 1965 in Bangalore. Given the expected difficulties in locating sample members ten years later, the rate of 31 per cent for a mail follow-up is not unusually low. Although the new data will be used with caution, we believe it does provide valuable longitudinal data on the lives of these highly educated women.

Comparative significance of the findings

The 1966 report of the Indian Education Commission, the D. S. Kothari Report (India, Ministry of Education, 1966 : 300) showed that Indian women are increasingly going for not only college education but also post-graduate studies.[11]   Looking at the enrollment in university education at all levels, the ratio of women to men rose from 10.9 per hundred in 1950-51, to 16.2 per hundred in 1960-61, to 21.9 per hundred in 1970-71. In fact, the gap between qualified men and women is declining more rapidly in higher education than at the school level (Indian Council of Social Science Research 1975 : 149).

Highly educated women, who are usually found in urban areas, are influenced in a particular way by currents of change.   Development in India, as elsewhere, has increased job opportunities for educated women while resulting in a general decrease in women's employment (Indian Council of Social Science Research, 1975 : 23; Youssef, 1976).   Here we are dealing with urban middle class women who have been exposed to higher education and who may or may not work outside of the home. The women and their families are confronted with choices and decisions about the appropriateness of their expanded set of roles, and about modifications of old roles.

To what extent can generalizations be drawn from this data to educated women in other parts of India?   The extensive interviews of North Indian women done by sociologists Rama Mehta (1970, 1975) and Promilla Kapur (1970, 1974) attest that many of the same processes and problems are being experienced by highly educated urban women elsewhere in the country. This occurs in spite of caste and regional differences in practices such as *purdah*, which affect women.

Certain changes will be most dramatic in big cities, but an interchange of persons between cities and villages takes place.   Bangalore's special characteristics as a southern city having a heterogenous population, as a former seat of the British, as an educational center, as a city to which industrialization came later than that of other major cities—have affected the rate of its change.   Bangalore women tend to be more conservative than those in Bombay, yet more prone to change than those in smaller South Indian cities, and certainly far different from those in villages. Yet, as 20 per cent of India's population is now urban, we can expect the city, as a center of change, to have eventual influence on the village.

It is reported, for example, that when a residential school for tribal boys was started in one village, the illiterate tribal parents insisted on one for girls. They feared that boys, once educated, would refuse to marry within the community if there were no educated girls (Government of India, 1974 : 263). The value of educating girls has evidently taken some root, although opinion about the desired level of their education certainly differs widely. At the same time it must be remembered that college educated women are a tiny group, and that although there is a lessening gap between the educational level of men and of women, the percentage of Indians with college degrees remains extremely small. According to the Indian Ministry of Education, 0.7 per cent of females and 2.8 per cent of males in the corresponding age groups were enrolled in undergraduate (arts, science and commerce) colleges in 1960-61. One per cent of males and 0.1 per cent of females were enrolled in professional undergraduate education; while 0.5 per cent of males and 0.1 per cent of females were in general and professional post-graduate studies at that time. These figures include both urban and rural India (India, Ministry of Education, 1966 : 100, Table 5.5). By 1971, 2.4 per cent of females were enrolled in university education at some level (Government of India, 1974 : 149).

The significance of this small segment of highly educated women is difficult to assess. As it grows, the actual number (rather than the proportion) of such women provides a pool of intellectual talent and role models. Certain Indian women intellectual leaders are keenly aware of the problems of their less educated sisters, and are appealing to the college-educated to help improve the lot of all (Wasi, 1971). More indirectly, the emulation of higher castes and classes means that the role changes experienced by members of these groups will be carefully observed. M. N. Srinivas, referring to the highly educated urban middle classes, maintains, "This section of Indian society is miniscule in size but its life-style is envied and admired by the others" (1977 : 234).

CHAPTER 2

SOCIAL AND ECONOMIC CHARACTERISTICS OF THE BANGALORE SAMPLES

Homes—an impressionistic survey

SUSHEELA is known to one of our research assistants by her reputation as an exceptionally beautiful and talented young Brahmin. She turns out to be of rather fair complexion (for South India), with large regular features, excellent diction, and great poise. Having overcome her widowed mother's objections to higher education she is now studying for a master's degree in English. Susheela lives with her mother and two elder unmarried sisters in a rather new but increasingly crowded residential area. Their house occupies its own plot among a row of similar small houses, none of which has a compound worthy of the name. Most do have a wall or fence surrounding their small piece of garden, and an entrance gate. This privacy of entry marks them as part of the middle class. Susheela greets us most cordially at the door and invites us into a small front room. Evidence of established middle class style is seen again in many tasteful decorative arrangements and wall hangings. The home is furnished with chairs and sofas, and we move into a second large room, definitely a mark of relative comfort. (Many houses we visit have but one small front room for entertaining visitors.) Susheela's father, now deceased, was a "superintendent", though it is not clear of what. His education, as well as her mother's, is that of a matriculate.[1] Family income is described as between 500 and 799 rupees per month and the young woman considers herself middle class. This designation is given in spite of the fact that her mother speaks English well and that Susheela pilots her own motor scooter to and from the University. Style of life might suggest upper-middle class status were it not for the family's income.

Farzana is a 24-year-old Moslem who has her master's degree in sociology, and is now teaching in a Methodist high school. Her address is one which our Hindu assistant cannot fathom. With the aid of a Moslem acquaintance (who herself lives in another part of Bangalore) we are able to locate the street in the congested and dirty Cantonment market area.[2] Inquiring at various shops we are directed to one where Farzana's father is working as a job typist. He turns out to be a military pensioner who cordially offers to take us to his home. As we encounter a neighborhood boy, however, Farzana's father turns the errand over to him and returns to work. The house is not far from the shop, a nondescript stone dwelling attached to others in a row, and fronting on the street. Neighborhood women gather around, explaining to us in Urdu that the girl's mother is dead and that the girl is a teacher and will be home on a particular day. These somewhat shabbily arrayed neighbors share the same house and each other's business, a characteristic seemingly more true of the less affluent because of their close contiguity.

Upon our return visit, we again meet Farzana's father, who apologizes for what he calls "our poor standard of living." Passing the cage of chickens in the hallway, we enter a very small neat apartment of two or three rooms which has been brightened up by a cheerful matching of curtains and pillow cushions. Farzana indicates that her father has a B.A. degree and was a lieutenant prior to being retired because of injuries. Her mother had finished middle-school.[3] Farzana has one brother and one sister, lists family income as between 300 and 499 rupees per month and she, too, calls herself middle-class.

Mary Sheela, a 22-year-old Christian B.A., seems similar to Farzana in economic circumstances. She is a clerk in the state government purchasing department and her father is a retired military mess manager, his education being "intermediate."[4] The mother, employed as a compounder of medicine in hospital, has finished her "Senior Cambridge." Mary Sheela has one sister, now married and living away from home. Our assistants found this house after difficulty, as it is set in from an alley which is off the main road. The land around it is low and damp, and animals roam in front of the door. A neighbour's child wanders in and out at will. We visit in the one main room, which appears to serve many purposes, and see a small kitchen further inside. Mary Sheela lets us know that she is helping to support the family, whose income is between 300 and 499 rupees per month, and she lists herself as middle-class.

Indira is a married 23-year-old Brahmin B.A. who has come back to her mother's home for the delivery of her first child. The mother and two younger sisters occupy a second-floor flat which is small but neat and tastefully furnished, in a Hindu residential area. The interview is held in the main room but we also get a chance to peep at the new baby swinging in a wooden cradle, in a small nearby room. Indira's father, now deceased, was an accountant who held a Bachelor of Commerce degree and a banking certificate. The mother's education is intermediate and she speaks excellent English. Indira lives in Bombay, in an independent household, with her engineer husband. She states that their income is between 500 and 799 rupees per month, and checks upper class to identify her status. Our assistant comments on this in her notes, as follows ; "She has written that she belongs to the upper class but this house was very modest. I can't decide anything because she lives with her husband." My own comment on this house, in comparison with others seen during the interviews, is "average."

Monica is a wealthy young Sindhi woman, age 22, who describes family income as well above 800 rupees per month, the point above which we did not ask for specific figures. Her house is large and extremely well-furnished. Like a few other homes visited by us it has a telephone, the mark of affluence in Bangalore. The area is a quiet one, but not new, and does not have the large compounds characteristic of some other areas. Monica has three brothers and five sisters, two of the latter living at home. The other sisters are living with their husbands, while one sister-in-law has been added to this household. Monica's father, the proprietor of a silk factory, has an intermediate education, while her mother lacks even a primary school education. Monica has not been allowed to continue past her bachelor's degree, for fear that she will expect a very highly educated mate. Her father is evidently seeking a bridegroom for her, but some candidates, otherwise promising, have not had auspicious horoscopes, which has caused delay. Monica would like to work but is not allowed to, and spends her days attending her ailing mother. She lists her class as upper middle.

Perhaps the most affluent home encountered was one that we did not get to enter. It is the family home of a young woman now residing in the United States with her engineer husband, who is working for an American firm. Mohini responded to a mail questionnaire after we were fortunate enough to obtain her address from a family member. Her parent's home is in a very wealthy section where Europeans prefer to reside and like others in the area, their luxurious compound is encircled by a high stone wall. Mohini's father is also an engineer and her mother is a college graduate. Family income is described as above 800 rupees per month, and Mohini is one of the four respondents calling herself upper class. While her name is of Sindhi origin, she writes only that she is Hindu and lists no caste designation.

These are impressionistic recollections of the varied homes and young women we encountered in 1966-67. Almost three-quarters of the interviews took place in homes—either those of the individual's parents or guardians, those of her in-laws, or her own nuclear household—affording ample opportunity to observe the range in dwelling places. Let us consider more systematically now some of the important background and family characteristics of the sample.

Caste, age, education and employment of respondents

As indicated in Table 1, the respondents are mostly single at the time of the original study. Seventy-five per cent of them are Hindu, 15 per cent are Christian, and 9 per cent are Moslem in 1967.[5] The corresponding figures for the 1977 follow-up group are 73 per cent, 20 per cent, and 7 per cent, respectively. The median age of both single and married respondents is 22 in 1967 and 32 in 1977. At the time of the first study, 44 per cent are employed, almost one-third are studying for advanced degrees, and about a quarter are neither working nor in school.[6] Originally we subtracted the number of young women seeking employment from this last group and estimated that less than 15 per cent of sample members would probably *not* enter the labor force. The possibility was considered that some of those still studying might not work, but this was thought unlikely. Ten years later we find that 20 per cent of those in the follow-up study have never worked. This figure may be slightly unrepresentative of the total sample since, as stated in Chapter 1, the follow-up includes a slightly larger proportion of women from higher income groups. There would be less economic need for them to join the labor force. Hence our original estimate is probably fairly accurate.

Our 1967 data pointed strongly to the supposition that acquisition of advanced degrees would lead to employment. As will be seen in Chapter 5, those who studied past an initial bachelor's degree are more likely to be currently working than those who did not. Five of the women who have never worked indicate that their husband, parents-in-law, or both preferred them to stay at home. The one single woman who has never worked states that she has been unable to find a suitable job.

The predominance of three major caste groupings in South India has been noted elsewhere, although nomenclature varies.[7] Theoretical disagreements regarding the most appropriate terminology to use in classifying India's hierarchical groups need not be of concern here [see, for example, Ghurye (1969 : Chap. 8) and Mandelbaum (1970 : Chap. 2)]. First, caste is not used as a major variable. Secondly, each respondent has no difficulty in naming her "community" or *jati*, the caste or sub-caste of which she considers herself a part. This community is an endogamous grouping, determined by birth, which serves as a source of identification for the individual and as a means of placement in the prestige hierarchy of such groups in South India.

TABLE 1—GENERAL CHARACTERISTICS OF THE BANGALORE SAMPLE

Variables		Number	Percent of total*
Marital Status			
Single		78	8
Married		19	20
Religion			
Hindu		73	75

Caste or community of Hindu	Number	Percent of Hindu
Brahmin	51	70
Non-Brahmin	18	25
Scheduled Castes	2	2
Other	2	2
Total	73	99

		Number	Percent of total*
Christian		15	15
Moslem		9	9
Present Status			
Now employed		43	44
Studying for advanced degree		29	30
Neither employed nor in school		23	24
Doing unpaid religious work		2	2
Age			
Median of sample		22	
Mode of sample		21	
Median of married respondents		22	
Mode of married respondents		22	

*Percentages in this and succeeding tables may not total 100 per cent, as figures are rounded. $N = 97$.

Brahmins are the only group that describe themselves by both caste and sub-caste names, such as Saraswat Brahmin.   They constitute about half of the sample and 70 per cent of the Hindus.   Most of those who are not Brahmins name their communities by one term, such as Bhandari, Nair, or Reddy, and not in terms of the four traditional *Varnas*.[8] Eighteen separate communities are among the non-Brahmins and none is represented more than twice.   One individual identifies herself as a *Kshatriya* and one as a *Vaishya*.   All of these are classified here as non-Brahmins, and they constitute 19 per cent of all respondents, or one-quarter of the Hindus. Two women are Sindhis and are classified in Table 1 as "other", since they do not give specific caste names.   The third major caste grouping of South India, the Scheduled Castes, or Harijans, are represented by only two individuals, or 2 per cent of the sample.   This percentage is interesting in light of the claim that compensatory legislation aiding "backward classes" has bordered on discrimination against Brahmins in Mysore State.[9]

While a few tables will provide some comparisons between Brahmins and other castes, it is obvious that most castes are not represented in numbers that would be significant for quantitative analysis.

Determining class status

One must agree with Rosen (1966 : 38) that "any attempt to define the middle class [in India] can easily become a morass."   However, while we need not go into the many complexities of class definitions, it is important to show that most respondents are accurately classified as middle class. This is necessary because class status enters into our analysis in a crucial way.

Data on income, own identification of class, education and occupation of parents, and type of dwelling quarters can be measured against the criteria of class presented by various authors.

Misra (1961 : 13) lists a wide range of occupational groups comprising the Indian middle classes, excluding from these all types of manual workers and also teachers below "the upper range" of secondary school teachers.   Only the highest range of government or business officials is considered to be above middle class.   Misra also includes as part of the middle classes, "the main body of full-time students engaged in higher education at a university or comparable level."   If we accept this criterion, then our respondents, all college graduates, are members of the middle class by definition.   What about their parents?

Rosen (1966 : 38-39) defines the urban middle class in terms of three groups, describing the type of occupational groups that fall into each stratum as follows :

On a top level, it is clear that the leading businessmen in India, the leading members of the government bureaucracy, and the leading intellectuals should be included. The higher income professionals, scientists and technicians, the professionals managers in industry, and the large merchants should also be associated with the upper group within the middle class. Below these are the mass of clerks and relatively minor officials in government offices and private commercial and industrial firms, the school teachers, working journalists, struggling professionals and the petty shopkeepers and possibly small-scale industrialists. Although this lower middle-class group generally has a high rate of literacy and education and an inclination toward white-collar jobs, individual incomes are low.

Note that Rosen does not distinguish an upper class from the upper range of the middle class.

The fathers of our respondents are engaged in a variety of occupations but, taking the largest possible estimate, not more than 9 per cent could be classified as lower or working class (see Table 2). Several hold permanent though low-paid governmental positions; the acquisition of higher education by their children indicates upward mobility.

There is no clear way of distinguishing, on the basis of occupation, between the very small elite upper class that some writers recognize and the upper level of the middle class. A man listed as "proprietor" may own a thriving business or a modest one. In the case of fathers described as "officials" the importance of their positions cannot be readily determined.

Middle-class mothers are not likely to have worked outside the home except in a very few types of jobs. Teaching and medicine are the most acceptable occupations for Indian women, and it is here that we find most of the mothers who have worked.[10] Of 11 mothers who are not, or were not, primarily housewives, three are physicians, one is a college teacher, five are school teachers, one does pharmaceutical work, and the last held a job in public transportation prior to her death. The two nonprofessional positions are held by Christians, among whom traditional norms against work are probably not as strong. In all, then, not more than 11 per cent of mothers have worked outside the home, and most in "respect-able" middle-class occupations.

TABLE 2—FATHERS' OCCUPATIONS

Occupations		Number	Percent
Professional and managerial	Total	69	70
Proprietor or landlord		14	14
Manager, supervisor or official		29	30
Doctor, lawyer or engineer		14	14
College teacher		4	4
Other professional		8	8
Semi-professional and white-collar	Total	19	20
School teacher		2	2
Semi-professional or technical		8	8
Clerical or white collar		9	9
Working Class	Total	9	9
Armed forces or police		4	4
Skilled worker or operative		2	2
Not given or not clear (a)		3	3
	Total	97	98(b)

(a) This table is intended to give highest possible estimate of working class families.

(b) Totals and sub-totals calculated separately and rounded.

Considering income as a criterion of class, Rosen (1966 : 189) divides the Indian middle class into three income groups : the upper-middle class, which receives incomes above Rs. [rupees] 12,500 per year, the middle-middle class with incomes from Rs. 3,600 to 12,500 per year, and the lower-middle class with incomes below Rs. 3,600 per year. He maintains that, during the decade 1951-1961, the number in the lower middle class "defined as white collar employees with incomes below Rs. 300 per month" increased by over 100 per cent. Thus the representation of people in the lowest stratum of the middle class can be expected to be quite large. According to Rosen,

A recent survey of the incomes of middle-class families in the four major cities of India—Calcutta, Bombay, Delhi, and Madras—shows that in 1958-59 the average monthly income of all families ranged from about Rs. 300 to about Rs. 380 per month, of which Calcutta had the highest average and Madras the lowest. About 60 per cent of the families had incomes below the average of Rs. 300 per month, with the maximum concentration in the range of Rs. 100-200 per month.

These income figures may be used for *rough* comparison with the income figures given by members of our sample in 1966-67.

As can be seen in Table 3, less than one-tenth of those studied report family income to be below 300 rupees per month, and almost three-fifths say it is between 300 and 799—putting them in the middle of the middle class according to Rosen's divisions. About one-third have family incomes of 800 rupees or more per month, a figure which Indian academic colleagues considered a rather comfortable income but which falls partly into Rosen's middle segment of the middle class. While a few respondents with high incomes may belong within the tiny elite upper class, less than a tenth of those in the highest income bracket so classify themselves. If we combine income with our evaluation of class position, only 3 per cent fall within the upper class (see Table 3).

TABLE 3—CLASS IDENTIFICATION BY FAMILY INCOME

Family income (in rupees per month)	Class Identification									
	Total		Upper		Upper Middle		Middle		Lower Middle	
	No.	%	No.	%	No.	%	No.	%	No.	%
Below 299	7	7	0	0	0	0	7	11	0	0
300-499	25	26	0	0	2	7	22	34	1	100
500-799	33	34	1	25	9	32	23	36	0	0
Above 800	32	33	3	75	17	61	12	19	0	0
Total	97	100	4	100	28	100	64	100	1	100
	100%		4%		29%		66%		1%	

Two criteria of class, father's job and family income, are related. The median income of those holding professional and managerial jobs is between Rs. 500 and 799; of those holding middle and lower level jobs, between Rs. 300 and 499 monthly.

A study by the National Council of Applied Economic Research in India (1972), made available since publication of our first book, considers as middle class in 1967-68 annual incomes from Rs. 5000 to 14,999. By this criterion, more than 7 per cent of the respondents were definitely below middle class economically.   Since the breaking points used differ, we do not know how many of the families earning between Rs. 300 and 499 per month fall above and below Rs. 5000 yearly.   The figures do suggest that higher education is becoming available to some women in the lower ranges of the middle class, and even to a few whose parents have not made it to the middle class.

The fathers of somewhat less that two-thirds of the sample are working. Three who are retired from their regular occupations and who have taken other jobs are included among the employed, but 16 per cent are retired and not working.[11] More than a fifth of the fathers, as contrasted with 8 per cent of the mothers, are deceased. Thus, due to death and retirement, more than one-third of the families are deprived of the regular income of a father.

Respondents were asked, "what class do you consider your family to be?" and given a choice of upper class, three levels of middle class, lower class and other. Ninety-five per cent of them chose the two categories within middle class called "upper middle" and "middle."[12]   These are the two major divisions perceived by respondents, and for some purposes we shall subsume the few "upper class" designees into the "upper middle class" group and the one "lower middle class" individual into the "middle class" category.

Referring to Table 3, we see that income and class identification are related.[13]   Three-quarters of those calling themselves "upper class," a little over 60 per cent of the "upper middle class," and less than 20 per cent of the "middle class" report incomes of Rs. 800 and above. All with incomes below Rs. 300 call themselves "middle class."   Yet it should be noted that almost one-fifth of those in the highest income group also consider themselves "middle class."   Respondents tend to evaluate their class position in economic terms but differ somewhat in their standards of judgment.

Ten years later, the lowest family income reported is between Rs. 700 and 999 monthly; only three women, or ten per cent, fall in this range. Two of them work and contribute substantially to family income. Both are married to men who have not been educated past the bachelor's degree. The third case of relatively low family income is that of a single woman with a B.A. degree who has not been able to find work. The median income of the sample is between Rs. 1500 and 1999 per month, while approximately 14 per cent have incomes of Rs. 3000 and above. One working respondent explains her high family income, writing in that two brothers are also employed and her father receives a pension. Because of the high rate of inflation, these income figures cannot be easily compared to either the 1967 figures or the 1967-68 standards used by the National Council of Applied Economic Research. However, it would appear that most of those reporting have managed to keep up a middle or upper-middle class standard of living commensurate with their own education or that of their husbands.

Both the living costs and the income of a family fluctuate over time. The number of children attending schools and colleges has a direct impact on family finances. The father is most likely to be the main source of financial support during the period that most of his children are being educated, meeting the costs of tuition and books as well as living expenses. However, once older brothers have finished college and obtained employment, family income may go up dramatically. The vast majority of respondents come from homes in which at least one sibling has completed his or her education. But at the same time, most have at least one sibling still in the process of being educated.

As an extreme example, in 1967 a Brahmin woman with seven well-educated elder brothers described how her family's financial status had changed, saying "All my brothers studied by getting scholarships and freeships. In fact we were poor and it was very difficult when my father died. But now all of them have come up." This respondent lists family income in the highest category, and class as "upper middle"—in spite of the fact that the family, including some married brothers, resides in small and modest quarters.

According to one study (United States, 1961 : 61), the type of dwelling unit is a relatively poor indicator of economic status, inasmuch as most of the Bangalore population lives in brick, stone or cement houses. Hut dwellers are relatively small in number compared to some other cities, and none of our respondents is included among this group. On the other hand, houses vary considerably both in interior furnishings and exteriors. As suggested in the beginning of the chapter, more modest dwellings are characterized by such features as : small number and size of rooms, little privacy from neighbours, external overcrowding of units, absence of gardens or compounds, absence of fences and gates, the presence of roaming animals close to the house and in some cases the keeping of chickens within the hallways. The well-to-do representatives of Bangalore society, whom foreigners tend to meet socially, possess more spacious compounds than almost all we encountered in the course of interviewing. We saw the exteriors of homes of three of the four respondents who call themselves "upper class"; only that of the young woman now residing in the United States, described earlier, resembles in affluence the most fashionable homes found in Bangalore.[14]

Most of the homes encountered had some kind of front room in which visitors could be greeted, but these varied greatly in furnishings and decor. A chair was almost always produced for the foreign visitor, but occasionally mats served for our Indian assistants. A range in living standards is obviously characteristic of the broad stratum considered to be a part of the middle class.

Because traditional attitudes toward women tend to be more restrictive among Moslems, it might be expected that highly-educated Moslem women represent a more westernized elite group. Personal visits to Moslem homes suggest otherwise, as does consideration of income and class. The majority of both Moslems and Christians place themselves in the "middle class"; the median income of both groups is between Rs. 300 and 499 although both exhibit a wide range. In general, then, some level of middle class status characterizes the non-Hindus as well as the Hindus.

We have looked at a number of indices of class : income, fathers' and mothers' occupations, own identification of class, and characteristics of dwelling place. Each by itself is not a conclusive indicator; taken together these facts provide overwhelming evidence that we are dealing with a middle class sample. To repeat our starting premise, college and graduate education is no longer the privilege of a small elite group but has now become available to the growing number of urban middle class women.

If it is true that many members of the middle classes feel economically pressed, the likelihood that a woman's education will lead to gainful employment is increased. Kapadia (1966 : 265) claims that this is happening :[15]

Under the pressure of economic necessity, opposition to the gainful occupation of women is steadily diminishing. The Second World War, and particularly the period after its close, hit the middle class so hard economically that this change in attitude is shown even by members of the older generation.

Educational attainments of parents and siblings

Respondents were quick to give very exact information on the educational level of their parents, except in a few cases where fathers apparently had little education.

Table 4 contrasts the education of fathers and mothers.[16]   Forty-seven per cent of the fathers, as contrasted with seven per cent of the mothers, had obtained one or more college degrees.   More than half of the college-educated fathers hold two or more degrees.   In contrast, looking at the lower levels of educational attainment, we find that only 7 per cent of the fathers but over 60 per cent of the mothers have not completed secondary school (tenth standard).

TABLE 4—FATHERS AND MOTHERS OF RESPONDENTS BY
EDUCATIONAL LEVEL

Highest level finished	Father		Mother	
	No.	%	No.	%
College	45	47	7	7
Secondary school (a)	44	46	28	29
Below secondary school	7	7	61	64
Total (b)	96	100	96	100

(a) Or specialized language or music education.
(b) One respondent did not provide this information.

The pattern of highly educated men being married to rather uneducated spouses is quite common in India.   However, of the seven college-educated mothers, six are married to men with degrees, suggesting that the reverse pattern is unlikely to obtain.   We will see that this generation's college educated women expect to marry at least equally well-educated husbands, and they consider that being a "graduate" aids in doing so, even though most of their mothers did not find education necessary.

When middle-class girls were married during childhood, their education tended to be discontinued.   In consequence, such females were not prepared for respectable work outside the home.   The 11 mothers who have worked constitute a more highly educated group, almost three-quarters of them having finished secondary school or above, as contrasted to one-third of all mothers who have done so. In addition, two have a specialized language education qualifying them to teach. Of the seven mothers holding a college or medical degree, five are working or have worked. The relationship of higher education to employment is apparently not a new phenomenon; more Indian women obtaining college degrees and hence becoming employed, is.

Considering the small percentage of Indian college graduates, the fathers represent a highly educated group. The mothers are more highly educated than the vast majority of Indian women in Karnataka State. More than one-third of them finished seventh standard approximately three decades ago, when female education was even less usual.[17]

However, the contrast between respondents and their mothers is sharp. One hundred per cent of the younger women and only 7 per cent of their mothers hold college degrees. The relationships between these highly educated daughters and their mothers might well be worthy of study. Furthermore, when and if they marry, these graduates will have to relate deferentially to mothers-in-law whose educational background will probably resemble their mothers'.

Although fathers' education is not significantly related to income, it does tend to be associated with class identificaton. If her father does not have a college degree, his daughter is much more likely to classify the family as "middle" rather than "upper middle" class.

More than half of the sample comes from families in which there are five or more children (see Table 5). While the median number of both brothers and sisters is two, there are slightly more sisters than brothers.[18] Eighty-two women have one or more brothers while 84 have one or more sisters; only three individuals have no siblings. The relationship between the number of siblings and caste or religion is not statistically significant. However, the families with more siblings have proportionately higher incomes than those with fewer siblings.[19] This fact is open to varying interpretations. Perhaps only large families which are also relatively well off can afford to keep their daughters in college. Or perhaps families with more children also tend to have some who are working and contributing to the household.

Educational information about brothers and sisters was given readily, in much detail as to type of degree, subjects studied and degree of merit attained. Since all but the poorest families send their children to some type of private school rather than to a government school, large families

TABLE 5—INCOME, CASTE AND RELIGION BY NUMBER OF RESPONDENTS' SIBLINGS

Number of siblings	Total		Income (in rupees per month)								Caste and Religion							
			Below 299		300-499		500-799		800 up		Brahmin		Other Hindu		Moslem		Christian	
	No.	(%)	No.	(%)	No.	(%)	No.	(%)	No.	(%)	No.	(%)	No.	(%)	No.	(%)	No.	(%)
3 or fewer	43	(44)	6	(86)	13	(52)	15	(45)	9	(28)	22	(43)	9	(41)	4	(44)	8	(53)
4 or more	54	(56)	1	(14)	12	(48)	18	(55)	23	(72)	29	(57)	13	(59)	5	(56)	7	(47)
Total	97		7		25		33		32		51		22		9		15	

mean a continuous financial commitment over many years. Tuition rates in private schools vary tremendously, from a high charged at the most exclusive English medium schools to the low at neighborhood schools. More than a quarter of the families have other children in attendance at both colleges and lower schools, another quarter or so have other children studying below college level only, and another quarter have no other children currently studying.

The quest for higher education appears to be a family decision rather than an individual matter. Forty-six respondents have at least one sister who holds a college degree; 45 respondents have at least one brother with a degree. About one-quarter of the sample have at least one brother and one sister who are college-educated.

Mobility through education

Eighteen individuals are the first members of their families, including their parents, to obtain a degree. How do they compare with the rest of the sample ? Perhaps the most striking difference is in fathers' occupations. Whereas 70 per cent of all fathers are classified in professional and managerial occupations (Table 2), only one-third of these fathers are so classified. Seven of the total of nine fathers designated as having working class occupations are found in this group. One-third of the Christian respondents are the first in their families to obtain degrees, while this is true of less than one-seventh of the Brahmins and one-ninth of the Moslems. While the modal income is the same, between 500 and 799 rupees monthly, 44 per cent of the "first to be educated" have monthly incomes below 500 rupees as contrasted to 33 per cent of the total. Seventy-eight per cent of this group call themselves "middle-class" (rather than upper middle class or above) as compared to two-thirds of the total. Of the nine mothers who are either working or have worked, four are represented among this group. Without going into greater detail as to the significance of these facts, it is obvious that the women who are first in their families to acquire an education come from lower socio-economic backgrounds than average and are upwardly mobile.

Marriage to highly educated men

Educational information about 19 husbands and one future husband turns up only one who lacks a college degree. Three have only a B.A.,

B.Sc. or other diploma, with the remaining 80 per cent having higher education or studying for advanced degrees. Eleven, or more than half, are doctors, lawyers or engineers, while four fall into the "other professional" category. Four are in the clerical or white collar group, while one is a manager. Thus, 80 per cent are in the professional or managerial class.

Respondents continued to follow the norm of marrying men who are at least as educated as they are. In the follow-up, four of the 25 husbands have only a B.A. or B.Sc. degree, while the remaining 84 per cent have advanced degrees. The same 84 per cent are professionals, managers or proprietors; the other husbands have jobs which appear to be semi-professional or technical. None of the women is married to a man with only a bachelor's degree if she has herself gone beyond a bachelor's. However, we included in these statistics one woman who is separated from her husband—she has a B.Ed. while he has a B.Sc.

Comparison of household types of Bangalore samples

Questions about the persistence or dissolution of joint family living have been a matter of debate and concern among social scientists, many of whom view the joint family as intimately related to other traditional patterns.[20] On the other hand, Shah (1974), in a thoroughgoing critique of literature on household composition in India, provides evidence for the historical existence of many household types. The data on composition of households presented here add to the factual evidence available on this question. However, questions were not asked about the pooling of income or other such indices of joint family life. To the extent that the joint family concept includes members not residing in the household, the joint family will be underrepresented in these figures. Shah disagrees with the assumption that urbanization causes a decline in joint family patterns. Among the numerous typologies which he finds flawed is that used by Ross (1961) in her first Bangalore study.

Nonetheless, interesting comparisons can be made between our two Bangalore samples and the follow-up group by using her typology, with certain modifications. As Ross points out, an individual may live in several types of family units during the course of his or her lifetime. Our data refers to the period in their lives represented by the average age of respondents.

Ross' classification is as follows: Type A is the large joint family, distinguished from Type B by its generational depth. It includes three or more generations living together in the same household, cooking in the same kitchen, owning property in common and pooling their incomes for common spending (Ross, 1961 : 34). A case is included in the Type A category if members of three or more generations are living together patri-locally, and regardless of whether or not there are additional relatives in the household.

As can be seen in Table 6, 16 per cent of our respondents, but none of the married ones, are living in Type A families.

Type B is the small joint family, defined by Ross (1961 : 35) as "com-posed of a household in which parents live with their married sons and other unmarried children, or two brothers live together with their wives and children." A family fitting this description may have one or more additional relatives in the household, but lacks more than two generations in depth. Thirteen per cent of the sample live in this type of household. A little more than one-quarter of the married women are living with in-laws in Type B families, but none of the seven mothers is doing so. Nine of the single women are living in small joint families.

Type C consists of the nuclear family, composed usually of one or both parents and their children. Almost three-fifths of the respondents live in such family units.

Shah points out that the concept of joint family frequently implies patrilocal residence. A widowed or divorced woman who goes back to live with parents or brothers (sometimes bringing children) would not be an accredited member of that household unit. It seems inappropriate therefore to represent this unit as a joint family. Ross solves this dilemma by creating Type D.

Type D : "the nuclear family with dependents consists of parents, their children and one or more dependents." A person is considered a depen-dent when he "has no authority or responsibility in family matters" (Ross, 1961 : 36). In setting up this category, Ross appears to have in mind such individuals as married sisters or widows living in a brother's home; a brother who is earning and contributing is likely to be considered a "true" household member. Thus, the presence of the earning brother would tend to make this a small joint family, Type B.

Here we shall deviate slightly from the above usage by including as a Type D nuclear family any one which has one or more odd relatives other than those in the nuclear unit living in the home. The distinction

TABLE 6—SINGLE, MARRIED, AND SEPARATED RESPONDENTS BY HOUSEHOLD TYPE

Family Type	Single				Married				Separated				Total			
	1967		1977		1967		1977		1967		1977		1967		1977	
	No.	(%)	No.	(%)	No.	(%)	No.	(%)	No.	(%)	No.	(%)	No.	(%)	No.	(%)
A (Large joint family)	15	20	0	0	0	0	0	0	0	0	0	0	15	16	0	0
B (Small joint family)	7	9	1	25	5	26	8	33	0	0	0	0	12	12	9	31
C (Nuclear)	41	54	3	75	13	68	10	42	0	0	0	0	54	57	13	45
D (Nuclear with dependents)	13	17	0	0	1	5	6	25	0	0	1	100	14	15	7	24
Totals (a)	76	100	4	100	19	99	24	100	0	0	1	100	95	100	29	100

(a) Of the two respondents not included in the 1967 totals, one is a nun living in a religious order, and the other gave no information; the one respondent not included in the 1977 totals is a nun.

between Type B and Type D is sometimes difficult to make, and when in doubt we classify the family as Type D. Thus, although a young woman may be earning and contributing to the household, she is still thought of as under the protection of her brother and dependent on him socially. Four single women, living in homes other than those of their own parents, are classified in Type D. Three cases occur in which brothers-in-law reside with their wives, sisters of our respondents, and in-laws. These men are appendages to nuclear families and are therefore classified as dependents. In seven additional families other relatives are living as dependents, so that this type of unit totals 15 per cent of the households.

Again, Shah shows that while the residing of men with their in-law families is not a preferred form, it does occur with some regularity. Since all family members interact in terms of prescribed norms, the presence of additional persons in the home adds to the complexity of interaction. Hence he prefers to use the term "complex" in referring to households which include more than one parental family.[21]

Considering that Ross' sample of Bangalore families was obtained in a different manner from the present one, and more than ten years earlier, the obvious similarities in data are noteworthy. Looking at Table 7, we see that almost half of her respondents and 57 per cent of ours report living in nuclear family units at the time of the initial study. Both samples show 16 per cent or less living in the large joint family, Type A. Type B is more prominent in the Ross sample, and is probably only partly accounted for by our difference in classification. Perhaps most significant is the prevalence of the nuclear household in both studies. Higher education makes spatial mobility more likely, and many husbands of respondents work in localities other than those of their parents. They may well be contributing to their parents' household financially and also entering into decision-making about important matters such as the marriage of sisters. In this sense, they are still a part of the joint family, even though they are not involved in day-to-day decisions.

The household composition of the 1977 respondents is presented for comparison. The percentage of those who live in nuclear families is less than those in both the original Blumberg and Ross samples. This is true especially of married respondents (see Table 6). Of the 19 married respondents in 1967, 13 or 68 per cent were living in Type C nuclear units. Of the 24 married respondents in the follow-up, only 10 or 42 per cent are in such units. While this latter figure must be used cautiously, it does

suggest that the nuclear household may be but one stage in a develop-
mental pattern, and not the result of a decline in traditionalism.   Those
living in either Type B or Type D families are 55 per cent of the total in
1977.   The practice of including other than nuclear family members in
households apparently persists.   The figures are particularly striking if it
is remembered, (as noted in Chapter 1), that almost half of the married
women responding to our 1977 questionnaire do not live in Bangalore.
The pressures for joint family living are greater when such residence is a
possibility.

TABLE 7– COMPARISON OF HOUSEHOLD TYPES OF BANGALORE
SAMPLES

Family type	Ross sample[a]		Blumberg samples			
	No.	%	1967		1977	
			No.	%	No.	%
A (Large joint family)	19	13	15	16	0	0
B (Small joint family)	44	28	12	13	9	31
C (Nuclear)	77	49	54	57	13	45
D (Nuclear with dependents)	17	11	14	15	7	24
Totals[b]	157	101	95	101	29	100

(a) Totals abstracted from Ross, Aileen B. (1961).   *The Hindu Family in Its Urban
Setting*, Table XIII, p. 303.

(b) Of the two respondents not included in the 1967 totals, one is a nun living in a
religious order; and the other gave no information.   The one respondent not included in the 1977 totals is the nun.

This typology, as many others, tends to obscure the complexity of
variations in household units.   On the basis of his study of a Gujarat
village, Shah suggests a dichotomy of "simple" and "complex" household
types. A simple household is a complete or incomplete parental family—
including only parents and unmarried children if complete.   A widow
living alone would be considered as living in an incomplete parental household.   A complex household includes more than one complete or incomplete parental units (Shah, 1974 : 13-14).

Families are most often considered joint when they follow the norm
which Shah calls "the principle of the residential unity of patrikin and
their wives." Wives are to be completely incorporated into their husbands'
kin group and, even after a husband's death, should stay on in the same

household.   However, in actual practice, this principle may be reversed, resulting in complex households in which a woman returns to her parental home, with or without husband and children.   At times a woman may take some members of her parental kin group into her conjugal home. Shah found seventeen complex households of this kind in the village he studied.   In four of those cases a widowed daughter or her children came to live with one or both of her parents.

Those who come to live in a household by a reversal of the principle of residential unity of patrikin are called by Shah "accretions," while others in the household are "core" members—somewhat similar to Type D-nuclear unit with dependents.   However, such units may be more than two generations in depth.   The accretions or dependents do live in the household and, in spite of deviating from the desired norm, are part of the complex interaction patterns of the home.   Four of the women classi-fied as in Type D in the 1977 sample are living in families of three genera-tions in depth, in situations which are a reversal of the principle of the residential unity of patrikin.   One of them has separated from her hus-band and returned with her children to live with her father, brothers and aunts.

Evidently there are many occasions when a widow returns to her parental home rather than staying with her in-laws as prescribed.   The divorced or separated woman may have even more reason for doing so. This was found to be a frequent practice by Rama Mehta (1975), in her study of divorced Hindu women.   She found that in the more sophisti-cated urban upper middle class divorced women experience less stigma and more acceptance by affinal relatives than in the lower middle class. The problem of satisfactory living arrangements for the single, widowed or divorced woman is a frequent theme of those concerned with women's status.[22]   In talking about the need for marriage, our respondents were aware that if they remained single they would most likely have to live with brothers and brothers' wives.   This topic will be discussed more thoroughly in Chapter 4.

Christians differ from other groups in the sample in that all but one of the families live in nuclear units, and that one is a "nuclear family with dependents."   While Moslems and Christians resemble each other in having slightly lower incomes on the average than the Hindus, Moslems also have a joint family system, comparable to that of the Hindus.   Income is slightly related to household type, but the relationship is not statistically significant.   The small joint families are more highly represented among those with higher incomes, while the nuclear families have a higher proportion of lower income households.   The small joint family often includes adult brothers and hence more contributors to family income.   Further study is needed to explore these relationships.

To sum up, the average woman studied in 1967 is single, 22 years old, comes from a highly educated middle class group, has four brothers and sisters, and has a family income between 500 and 799 rupees per month; in addition, she is more than 50 per cent likely to reside in a nuclear family unit, 44 per cent likely to be employed, and almost 33 per cent likely to study for an advanced degree.

Of the 31 per cent included in the ten-year follow-up, the average woman is 32 years old, and reports a median family income between Rs. 1500 and 1999 per month.   In comparison to 1967, she is less likely to live in a nuclear family.   She is married to a man with an education at least equivalent to her own and is equally likely to be employed or staying at home.

CHAPTER 3

STUDENTS IN SARIS : THE MEANING OF EDUCATION

Women's right to education linked to family status

WOMEN'S right to education has been, throughout the world, a question of debate and struggle. Most often the argument is supported by those who see illiterate and ignorant women as poor wives and mothers—women who cannot socialize their children to new values. Lacking education, women are said to cling to tradition.[1] Thus, particularly in times of national freedom struggles, women's education and women's rights assume importance. India's case illustrates this well; amelioration of the status of women was included as an important goal of the Independence Movement.

Once education has been won as a right, women's access to it may be achieved unevenly, level by educational level. Cultural beliefs as well as material conditions influence the attainment of this goal. In the mid-sixties, the ratio of Indian female to male students in higher education was 1:4, a figure closely resembling that in the Sweden of 1952-53 (Degler, 1964 : 202). Yet, illiteracy is still a real problem in India. The over-all literacy rate is rising slowly, but that of females is still less than half that of males (Government of India, 1974 : 155).

Progress is uneven and difficult to assess. In the United States, for example, women constituted almost 40 per cent of the students in institutions of higher learning in 1937, but decreased to 35 per cent in 1952-53 (Degler, 1964 : 202).

Women's education is closely linked with their status in the family and in society as a whole, as suggested in the following passages. Lamb (1966 : 159) considers the status of Indian women to be an unhappy one, stating:

Although her legal position has been greatly improved, the Hindu woman, except in Westernized circles, is still bound by ancient traditions of behavior that emphasize her submission, obedience, devotion, and absolute dedication to her husband and his every wish. Her husband is almost a god, and the home is her life and her career... Among the tiny emancipated Westernized minority, there are many outstanding and forceful women prominent in public life... But such women are the exceptions. The vast majority are far less educated than the Indian men. In 1961, the rate of literacy among women was less than half that among men. Because women still generally follow tradition, successive generations of Indian children—even those of Westernized fathers—learn the old values and modes of thought from the womenfolk who bring them up. This is another reason for the tenacious hold of many old customs and for the continued coexistence of the new and old.

Writing at the same time, the Indian sociologist, K. M. Kapadia (1966: 266-267) paints a more optimistic picture:

The rapid strides in higher education during the last twenty-five years have exercised their impact in two ways, first by creating conditions for a woman to be self-reliant and secondly by creating stronger emotional bonds between her and her husband. An educated young man is no longer satisfied with the prospect of a wife who can only be the acquiescent slave of his desires and the begetter of his children, but looks for intellectual cooperation and participation in the pleasures and joys of life. The educated wife is expected to be a companion who will share his interests, go with him to clubs and films, sports and parties, and thus be united emotionally with him. The new concept of wifehood, which is associated with urban living, has assigned to the wife a new status in the family, even if it be joint.

In a culturally biased view, which equates Westernization with progress, Lamb nevertheless justifies women's right to education on the basis of their role as mothers. Kapadia indicates that men are now seeking wives who are on a par with them educationally. In both cases, education or its lack is assessed in terms of its compatibility with women's traditional family roles. This should not be surprising. In India, as in many other countries, the marriage of daughters is of prime concern to the family. A women's other aspirations, and her behavior, are judged in terms of how they will affect her chances (and those of her sisters) for making a suitable match. Goals such as education take a second place, even though a few exceptions to this traditional emphasis can be seen. Hence the linkages between education and the marriage system are extremely important.

Here, however, we also focus on the meaning of education to young women themselves, and how they view its effects on their lives. Going to college is a highly valued activity, and further education the goal our res-

pondents are most willing to express.   When asked what they would like
to do in the next two years, given absolutely free choice, they most frequently mention educational aims.   In actuality, 30 per cent of the original sample are engaged in study for higher degrees at the time of the initial study, with an additional 28 per cent hoping or planning to continue
their education.   Of the remainder, almost one-third already hold higher
degrees.   In all, less than three-tenths of the sample definitely expect
to complete their education with only a bachelor's degree.[2]   (Ten years
later, we find that a slightly larger per cent, four-tenths of the follow-up
group, have not been educated past the bachelor's degree.)   Table 8
shows separately the educational aspirations and activities of the less and
more highly educated respondents.

TABLE 8—EDUCATIONAL LEVEL OF RESPONDENTS BY CURRENT
ACTIVITIES AND PLANS

| | Total | | Present Educational Level | | | |
| | | | Less Educated[a] | | Highly Educated[b] | |
	No.	%	No.	%	No.	%
Now studying for advanced degree	29	30	27	40	2	7
Planning to do further studies	27	28	13	19	14	50
Not planning further studies	40	42	28	41	12	43
Total	96	100	68	100	28	100

(a) "Less educated", in terms of present educational level, includes those holding
only a B.A. or B.Sc.

(b) "Highly educated" includes those who hold master's, double-bachelor's, medical,
and law degrees.

Given traditional notions of duty and obedience, the women's strong
and open commitment to education could not have occurred without the
support of family and community members.   To ascertain which of these
had been most influential, we asked, "Which family members have most
strongly influenced decisions about your education ?" Fathers alone, or in
combination with other family members, are designated almost two-thirds
of the time.   Mothers are named slightly less than two-fifths of the time,
and brothers are third in influence. In almost half of the cases, more than
one family member had strongly influenced decisions, showing that the

daughter's education is often a matter for family discussion.   Seven per
cent of respondents claim that continuing their education was their own
choice, without specific influence from others.

This strong family encouragement suggests that higher education may
now be viewed as a help rather than a hindrance in marriage, at least by
these families.   A Bangalore "graduate," visiting her kinship group in a
village, is still likely to face the conservative attitudes and suspicion that
attach to an educated woman.   But in the main she believes that college
education is more likely to help her in obtaining a mate than not, or at
least that it will not affect her marriage chances negatively.   Chapter 4
discusses her reasoning in more detail, but Table 9 shows the responses,
by educational level, to the question, "Do you think that education helps
or hinders in finding a suitable partner ?"   The less educated respondents
have a slightly more favorable opinion about the role of education in
marital choice.[3]

TABLE 9—WOMEN BY PRESENT EDUCATIONAL LEVEL AS THEY
VIEW ROLE OF EDUCATION IN FINDING A MATE

Role of Education	Total		Less Educated		Highly Educated	
	No.	(%)	No.	(%)	No.	(%)
Helps	60	(63)	47	(68)	13	(50)
Hinders	8	(8)	3	(4)	5	(19)
Neither; or, sometimes helps, sometimes hinders	27	(28)	19	(28)	8	(31)
Total	95	(99)	69	(100)	26	(100)

Modifications of norms about female education

The early advocates of "female education" suffered much criticism; today its opponents are considered old-fashioned and are fewer in number.
To understand why, one needs to examine a number of factors : changed
conditions facilitating education; the intermeshing of the education and
marriage systems; and the ways that traditional norms become modified.
While education may now be looked upon more positively, there is no
unanimity about how *much* education is desirable.

In the past, a number of interrelated norms about women's nature,
their relationship to men, and the need for marriage prevented women

from acquiring an advanced or even modest education. Among those to be considered are : the compulsory nature of marriage for women, the notion of women's perpetual tutelage and extreme sexual vulnerability, and the requirement of male protection. More general values, such as the importance of gossip and reputation, and the notion of individual nature are also relevant.

Reforms aimed at improving women's position, especially raising the marriage age, have had important consequences for education. Given changed conditions—daughters as yet unmarried in their teen years, the availability of inexpensive university education, and the increasing demand for educated brides,—some of the norms referred to above begin to get modified. The lack of alternatives to college attendance and the intrinsic value of education to young women also facilitate change. The greatest impediment to the education of girls was child-marriage, as Thomas (1964 : 315-316) indicates in this passage :

> As long as child-marriage was the general rule, it was difficult to make any appreciable progress towards the spread of female education, as among the better classes of Hindus, girls were married before they were old enough to learn the three Rs, and the lower classes were not interested in female education. But in 1929, the Prohibition of Child-Marriage Act . . . raised the minimum age for marriage of girls to fourteen. Once the old convention, that a girl had to be married before menstruation, was overcome, marriage did not always take place at the age of fourteen; in fact girls grew into young ladies of seventeen or eighteen before marriage proposals started coming in, and all that the parents could do, in the meantime, was to let their daughters continue their studies till marriage. And it even became fashionable for parents, whose daughters were remaining for want of desirable proposals coming in or for want of cash to provide dowry, to give out the plausible explanation that the girls were so passionately fond of their studies that it was impossible to put ideas of marriage into their heads.

Thus, as Thomas points out, the abolition of child marriage was a crucial factor in opening up the alternative of education to the female child. Without the deadline of puberty, fathers could pursue a more leisurely course in obtaining bridegrooms for their daughters. The high cost of marriages and dowry, coupled with other economic pressures, tended to push the marriage age up, and education could provide the justification.

Tradition had held that the only sure way of protecting a girl's chastity was to marry her off before puberty. Postponing marriage and providing her with more education might make a girl intractable, and less able to adjust to her husband and in-laws. However, the tradition of child marriage and one of its unfortunate consequences, child-widowhood, was to come under attack by certain reformers. Altekar (1962 : 62) maintains that "secular causes" or conditions also favored raising the age at marriage and that some members of the "advanced middle classes" had already adopted this practice before the 1929 passage of the Sarda Act.[4]

Whatever the secular causes, which Altekar does not describe, a long list of illustrious reformers provided ideological support for the Act. Individuals and groups continued their vigorous condemnation of child marriage after the law's passage, cognizant that the law alone did not insure change. Reformers not only pointed out the cruelties involved in child marriage, such as high maternity and infant mortality rates and the curse of early widowhood,[5] but they also stressed its impact on female education. Recalling more glorious days in Indian history, feminist leaders such as Annie Besant (1913 : 201-202) deplored the state of ignorance into which Indian women had fallen. The uneducated (often illiterate) narrow and provincial mother, through her strong family influence, was said to hamper desired social changes. Mahatma Gandhi (1942) castigated those men who would marry child-brides as motivated by lust, and counselled young men to disobey parents who would force them into such marriages.

Gandhi tied the amelioration of women's condition to the national welfare. Raising the age at marriage and improving the education of women became inseperable from other major goals, such as the abolition of *sati*,[6] the mitigation of caste inequality, and the gaining of national independence.

Advancement of marriage age and its consequences :
the need to "fill in time"

There is no doubt that reform in marriage age has come about, especially in cities. In Bangalore, middle class Brahmins, the caste group most orthodox in these matters, no longer feel obliged to marry their daughters before puberty. Less than one-fifth of the respondents, whose median age is 22, are married. Looking at those in the follow-up, five-sixths are married, the median age at marriage being 24.

Young women's views about the desirability of later marriage will be discussed in Chapter 4. While the rise in age at marriage is less dramatic in rural areas, it has occurred. According to the 1961 census, 77.7 per cent of rural girls of age 10 to 14 had never been married. The corresponding figure for urban girls was 93.1. By 1971, the percentage of rural girls in this age group who had never been married rose to 87.2; that of urban girls to 95.8.[7] Table 10 shows the percentage distribution of ever-married persons according to sex and age in 1961 and 1971.

TABLE 10—PERCENTAGE DISTRIBUTION OF EVER MARRIED
PERSONS ACCORDING TO SEX AND AGE, 1961 AND 1971

| | Rural | | | | Urban | | | |
| | 1971 | | 1961 | | 1971 | | 1961 | |
Age Group	Male	Female	Male	Female	Male	Female	Male	Female
10-14	5.31	13.79	7.92	22.37	1.50	4.21	2.04	6.99
15-19	21.06	63.09	43.50	85.80	7.38	36.24	26.90	70.60
20-24	55.91	93.78	60.75	95.54	32.78	80.90	41.08	87.28

SOURCE : *Towards Equality* : *Report of the Committee on the Status of Women in India,* p. 80.

It is interesting to note that the percentage of urban women who were married by age 24 decreased from 87.28 per cent in 1961 to 80.90 per cent in 1971. The age of marriage of our sample members fits in with the trend toward later marriage.

Given this new pattern, it is obvious that the middle class urban woman who graduates from high school at about 15 or 16 years of age has a gap of time to "fill" before marriage.

Further, the physically mature young woman is expected to keep herself from thinking about marriage. The relationship between Indian husband and wife has traditionally been sex-centered. Women are presumed to have strong sexual instincts, which must be ignored or repressed until they are married.[8] The motto, "An idle mind is the Devil's companion," was quoted by both Christian and non-Christian respondents, as they discussed the need for women to "keep busy." Keeping fully occupied would allow a young woman little time for thoughts of sex and marriage.

The problem of filling in time between high school and marriage can be solved if a young woman continues her education. A number of authors have commented on this.   Ross (1971 : 229) explains :

Perhaps one of the main reasons for this new trend is that, with the
change from child to adult marriage, the leisure time of girls must now
be filled in up to nineteen or even twenty-five years.   And college is one
way of 'keeping them busy' until marriage.

Mehta (1970 : 36) makes the same observation about another group of
women, saying that they went to college as an "accident" rather than as
part of a plan :

They continued their education because there was really no alternative
except marriage.   Since marriage at the age of fifteen or sixteen was not
an acceptable alternative to their fathers, the logical thing was to send
them to college.   Also, the small family unit of their parents did not
have the same means to keep the adolescent occupied as in a large family.

But the interaction between education and marriage is mutual.   Once
education is valued, marriage may be postponed.   Kapadia (1966 : 165)
suggests the proper age for marriage to be one which enables a young
woman to first complete college :

Education has become necessary for a female not only for marriage but
for her economic independence.   A college education is desired if the
female is to be a worthy partner in marriage.   Girls do not generally
matriculate before the age of 16.   Granting at least four years for a
college education, a girl would not be ready for marriage before 20, and
hence this is a desirable age for marriage.

Liberation from male chaperonage

However, a young woman's attendance at college involves leaving her
home and the chaperonage of her family, even if only for several hours a
day.   Underlying notions about women's need for protection are strong,
even though orthodox forms of *purdah* have been more prevalent in North
than in South India.   Fathers and male relatives have a religious duty to
protect the women of the family.   Altekar (1962 : 328) explains :

As a woman herself has observed in the Mahabharata, to be without a
proper protector is a great calamity of the fair sex in this world, which
is full of wickedness.   Manu therefore ordains that the father ought to
protect a woman while she is a maiden, the husband when she is married,
and the sons when the husband is no more; a woman ought not to re-

main independent. In the immediately next verse Manu points out that the father would be to blame if he does not marry his daughter in the proper time, the husband, if he does not look after his wife properly, and the son, if he does not protect his mother during her old age.

How is it then, that young women are allowed to go out into the world without a male protector? In our earlier book we observed that the norm about chaperonage and male protection was in a transitional stage in Bangalore. Certain compromises were being allowed in order that education could be obtained. However, the same woman who travelled to college alone might be restricted from attending recreational events alone. Some of the women studied were permitted to attend the cinema only if accompanied by a male relative. Many truly feared travelling alone. There was little disagreement among observers that a woman who did so would be subject to teasing, harrassment or worse. The most frequent substitute for a male chaperone, and one that young women seem to prefer as less restrictive, is the company of classmates or friends. Upon the senior author's return visit to Bangalore in 1977, many informants commented that the norm of chaperonage had become more relaxed. They felt that college students had greater freedom in moving about. This was the observation, too, of the junior author, who resided in Bangalore during most of the intervening ten years. Perhaps, symbolically, women's dress has become less uniform, and some young women can be seen wearing slacks rather than saris.

Only a few respondents admit that their parents object to co-education at the graduate school level. Remarks such as, "They trust me" or "They know I know right from wrong", suggest that the college educated woman is beginning to be accorded a certain amount of independence from male protection.

Just as the advantages of college education appear to outweigh traditional concerns about chaperonage, so there are indications that a good job, such as that of college lecturer, can entice women to travel daily by public transportation. It works the other way too : distance from home can determine whether or not a daughter will be permitted to take a particular job or attend a particular college. Here the relative conservatism of the family enters into the decision. For families are very concerned about their reputation, about what people will say. The effects of education or employment on marital chances are frequently judged in terms of community sentiment.

Community sentiment as social control and support for change

Classical theories about the anonymity of urban life fail to take into account societies such as India, which have close-knit endogamous communities—*jatis*, or caste groupings. The circle of individuals who are involved in and concerned about the activities of a particular family may be relatively small. Members of the endogamous community know and gossip about one another; gossip may affect family reputation. Girl-watching is practised not only by boys, but by elders and neighbors of all kinds. Since the good reputation of the woman is essential in making marriage arrangements, fear of gossip is strong. In the process of locating mates for their children, parents or third parties make many inquiries about potential candidates. Thus the importance of hearsay is great, especially since some families may falsify the information advanced about their marriageable children.

The comments of neighbors, friends, and community members serve not only as character references but may also carry weight in decision-making. Neighbors may enter into the process of convincing the family of a contemplated course of action, including that of sending a daughter to college. To the extent that the social climate favors higher education for women, the family will be encouraged to educate its girls. A "love marriage" known to be under discussion for over a year was finally permitted by the widowed mother of the man involved, after age peers had convinced her it was the wise thing to do. This case demonstrates that friends and neighbors can sometimes provide support for a potentially unpopular decision. The mother who agreed to an intercaste "love marriage" had already received assurances that she would be supported rather than criticized.

A somewhat similar case was described to the senior author during the follow-up study. A delay in decision-making may afford time for various factions to mobilize support, and for the family decision-maker to assess the support for different positions. If a decision involves modification of norms, such as permitting an intercaste marriage, its potential for disruption may be tested in this way.

The maintenance of position is, of course, involved in concern about reputation. The hierarchical nature of Indian society affects non-Hindus as well as Hindus. Each marriage must be arranged with extreme care as to its suitability. Individuals are matched in terms of caste, education, and sometimes class. The prospective bride's looks and her accomplishments in homemaking, music and other arts are taken into account while the man's education and occupation are most important. An unequal marriage is much talked about and casts a reflection on the family status. However, a marriage may be equal or unequal in various ways.

Educational equivalence as a factor in match-making

Women are expected to marry men who are at least as highly educated and preferably better educated than they are. Srinivas (1977 : 233) reports that among the urban educated middle class there is a tendency to permit marriages among the many South Indian Brahmin *jatis*—groups which were formerly endogamous. By reinterpreting the *jati* to include cognate *jatis*, the field of potential marriage partners is widened. This is particularly important for highly educated women if their own community is one which has few highly educated men. It is apparently more acceptable to widen the endogamous unit than to insist on marriages which are deemed unsuitable in terms of the relative education of man and woman. Here the traditional notion of "suitability" of match is brought to bear in requiring educational equivalence rather than rigid endogamy.

As pointed out in the passage by Thomas referred to previously, a girl's strong interest in education may be functional for both herself and her parents. Any delay in arranging her marriage can be ascribed to the daughter's passionate interest in learning. If the father is having difficulty in arranging a match, his daughter may conveniently request a delay in order to continue her studies. On the other hand, should a good match be found there is every likelihood that it will be made immediately. At least seven of the 18 married respondents finished their degrees after marriage. If chances for marriage become increasingly slim, the daughter may provide a face-saving device for her father by publicly indicating her deep devotion to a career or her lack of "a feeling for marriage."

The notion of individual nature as a "safety valve"

A society which has strong prescriptions about family roles must also provide safety valves. The notion of "individual nature" appears to serve such a purpose, by allowing for deviation from prescribed roles. This concept includes more than temperament or personality, and recognizes a unique aspect of every individual.

The existence of differences in individual nature are recounted in stories

of famous Indian women.   These heroines are described as colorful and
sometimes willful people who manifest their own distinctiveness while outwardly adjusting to the wishes of others. For example, the modern Indian
heroine, Saroj Nalini is described in her husbands's biographical account
as a dutiful wife as well as a strong personality (Dutt, 1929). (This also
suggests that within women's formally prescribed roles there are opportunities for more or less effective role-playing, and that "superwomen" have
existed throughout history. The superwoman plays many roles and plays
them well.)

Respondents allude to individual nature as a factor which must be taken
into account in family decisions about their daughters. The concept is
employed in references to the type of job or husband suited to a particular
woman, her willfulness or meekness, and her suitability for marriage.   It
is also used when referring to the wife's duty to adjust to her husband's
nature. A woman who is considered "strong-willed" will often be able to
exert more influence on her own fate than can a more timid sister.   One
who is intent on further education may be able to convince her parents to
permit it. If other community members disapprove, the parents can point
to their daughter's strong and persisting desire for it, to her nature.

Pursuit of advanced education

Because education is a respected and respectable value, young women
may show some boldness in asking parental permission to continue.   In
the following two cases, different degrees of persistence bring about different results. Two young Brahmins, one successful and the other unsuccessful in her quest for graduate education, describe their attempts in this way :

Mother was very much against my studying in a co-educational college.
That's why she didn't want me to study for my M.A. It took me a year
to convince her. My family is quite old-fashioned. My mother felt that
if I went to a co-educational college there would be functions which I
might have to attend, and the problem of transport, and a lot of undesirable things. I might be dropped home by boys, or have boys to the
house. She's very much against mixing with boys. But fortunately,
she got me my own conveyance (a motor-scooter) so now I can be completely independent.

In contrast, the unsuccessful woman states :

I wanted to continue but somehow my parents weren't in favor of it.

They preferred that I get married instead. I was very keen on doing an M.B.B.S. (medical degree). I was first class when I matriculated and was accepted for M.B.B.S. but they wouldn't allow . . . . A first, every time I thought of the M.B.B.S. I felt so bad, but now I am beginning to adjust. I am quite meek and I will do what my parents say . . . . Many girls will do what they want, but I am not that way.

These young women were interested in obtaining advanced degrees, a choice often seen as more problematic by parents than allowing their daughters to study for first degress. For, apart from early marriage, there are few alternatives to "putting" a daughter in college. Appropriate employment opportunities for less-educated girls are extremely limited, and young high school graduates would be considered too vulnerable to be permitted to work away from home. Household tasks, music lessons and needlework cannot fill all of the daughter's time. As the acquisition of the degree gains more prestige in the marriage market, college becomes a desirable and visible way of occupying time. The cost of college education is not exhorbitant and the middle class family, accustomed to paying tuition for secondary education, comes to think of it as an expected burden. The student can live at home, and as long as she returns at the proper hour, she may be presumed to have spent the day safely at college. Later the parents are faced with the question of whether or not their daughter should be allowed to continue for post-graduate work or to take a position. They know that a post-graduate is more likely to be educated out of the marriage market than a simple graduate; yet, if a husband has not yet been found, the easiest course once again is more education. The young woman is usually willing to accept this solution.

Since the female is not actively involved in seeking her mate, her own attitudes toward education need not be tied to considerations about marriage. She is expected to maintain disinterest in marriage until it is upon her. Asked whether they would advise the hypothetical sister of a friend to enter college, 85 per cent of the respondents give unconditionally positive responses. The following is a spontaneous description of what college life means to one Indian girl (mentioned just previously as unsuccessful in her desire to pursue a M.B.B.S. degree) :

College is the best part of our lives. We are so free to move with people. We get ideas, our minds are broadened. There is much to adjust to in college and we learn to adjust. It is good for us. We can see our friends every day. Now my friends are working or taking post-graduate work, and we don't see each other very much. They live far from me. But in college it's so exciting. It's the best time of our lives, I feel. Now this is different, this studying at home. I told you I don't go to the cinema very much. Many girls go. But I am allowed only to go with a member of the family . . . . My father never goes. My mother doesn't go out much. If some of the family is visiting I may go. Otherwise, my father doesn't allow me to go with other girls. He is quite orthodox.

Clearly, the woman who has attended college finds "sitting at home" a highly uninteresting prospect. This need not imply that she is career-oriented or even interested in the subjects she is studying. As is true in other countries, young women have mixed motivations for attending college. The following frank confession was made by a young lady who is now a college lecturer :

I only became interested in zoology after taking my M.Sc. My father wanted me to get married right after my B.Sc., but I didn't want, so I took up the M.Sc. But I was not interested in the subject. I only went to college to have good times, and many of us did. I had no thought of continuing, so I thought, if I get a third class, it's good enough. I thought that I would never use my education. I was lucky enough to get a second class, so I got a place and could go on.

Attendance at college, then, has certain intrinsic attractions in the form of greater freedom, the opportunity to see friends each day, and to have "good times." The results of this inquiry do not tally with that of Ross (1969 : 181), who claimed that Bangalore women attend college for two main reasons : to increase their marriage chances, and to relieve boredom. It is agreed that the young woman tends to find staying at home "boring" after she has experienced college. But these data suggest that further education may be preferred to some proposed match. The motivations of parents and their daughters must be differentiated; the parents may consider education an appropriate time-filler until a suitable mate is found, but the young woman may hope for a few more years of freedom before settling down to the wifely role.

Ross (1969 : 181) found that young women were less interested in college and studied less than did their male counterparts. While this may be partly because success in college is crucially related to man's instrumental role as breadwinner, other factors may also come into play. Women may not have to study as diligently as the particular male students with whom they are in competition. The most able and affluent young men will most likely specialize in medicine and engineering, regardless of their interests, and will probably not attend liberal arts colleges. Medicine and engineering are not as available to women, and liberal arts colleges are considered more appropriate for them. Hence these institutions undoubtedly attract some women with more ability than their male fellow students. Furthermore, without going into the historical reasons for this, the quality of teaching at some Indian colleges may leave something to be desired. The young instructor previously quoted pointed out that she developed interest in her subject in spite of the poor way in which her classes had been taught.

The women in the follow up study were asked whether they were able to achieve in education what they had aspired for. A little over 60 per cent of those responding replied in the affirmative.[9] Seven per cent were only partially content, and the remaining 33 per cent said they had not been able to achieve their educational objectives. Several stated that they had been prevented from going on for higher degrees by marriage, family opposition or family circumstances. Three of these respondents had hoped to study for doctoral degrees.

Women are sometimes permitted an education as a preparation for homemaking. The major fields of study chosen by members of our sample can be examined to see if this appeared to influence their choice. There are, of course, a number of factors limiting the choice of major. Certain "combinations" such as English and social science, or botany and zoology are offered together as majors. Too, the student has already made a choice between arts and sciences during her secondary school career and is likely to continue in the same general area. Her choice of college major and of graduate work is likely to be limited to what is offered at a local college, if this is the one her parents have chosen. As an example, one respondent who professed interest in psychology was not allowed to attend an out-of-town college where it was offered, and settled for sociology for her master's degree—a not unusual compromise elsewhere, such as in the United States!

It is interesting that almost half of the respondents report sciences or mathematics as the major subjects studied for their first degree, while a little over 40 per cent majored in English or social sciences. Only 10 per cent majored in home science (home economics), the field which would best prepare them for homemaking, and 2 per cent took a degree in medicine.

Of those taking second degrees, the largest number (34 per cent) have selected mathematics and science. The next field in popularity, accounting for a little more than a quarter of the group, is education, with English and social sciences almost as popular. To qualify for better teaching posts, a bachelor of education degree is frequently taken after the bachelor of arts or bachelor of science degrees. As teaching is considered the most appropriate work for young women, this interest in obtaining an education degree is not surprising. However, those who go on for master's degrees in science, social science or English will eventually qualify for the post of college lecturer. Although it is unusual, a third class master's degrees may even qualify one for such a job. A Christian acquaintance we knew, who held a third class degree, was hired as a lecturer by a Christian college. Major fields other than those mentioned above (home science and law, e.g.) account for 11 per cent of the sample members acquiring advanced degrees.

Advanced study does not appear to be associated with income. Forty per cent or more of the young women in each income category have already obtained higher degrees or are now studying for them. Five of the seven women with incomes below 300 rupees per month are in this more highly educated group, the largest percentage for any of the income categories. For such families, the woman's education is likely to be a way of bettering its economic circumstances. But how does one account for the fact mentioned earlier, that less than 30 per cent of the sample expect or want their education to end with the bachelor's degree? Our interpretation is that college-going produces its own impetus for continuing—as the most natural thing—once the initial degree has been attained, and if a husband has not been found.

The nexus between education and marriageability

Increased education may have diminishing returns as far as the marriageability of an Indian woman is concerned. Those who have done research on the subject hold different viewpoints about the degree of education considered desirable, but the disagreement may be related to when the study was done. The question is, how educated a wife does an educated man want? In a study done more than 15 years before our initial one, Margaret

Cormack (1961*a* : 49) draws the line at matriculation :

> The tradition is growing that 'a girl must go to school if she wants a chance for a good marriage.' Hence even modern education remains, for the Hindu girl, a road to marriage. All informants agreed that a girl betters her marriage chances by going up to Matriculation [roughly the the equivalent of high school] but that increasingly the penalty of higher education is the decrease of marriage chances.

Kapadia's viewpoint, that college education is valuable in the marriage market as well as essential for women's independence, has already been cited. Ross (1969 : 187) notes the growing acceptance of education but maintains that there is a residue of fear and resistance to it :

> It is . . . probable that on the whole there is still much more resistance to higher education for women (in India than elsewhere). Many Indians stiil see it as useless luxury, as it is not expected to be an asset to a married woman, and marriage is still their chief goal . . . . Western parents are . . . aware that eligible husbands may be found through co-education, whereas the Indian parent is afraid that co-education may possibly end in a dreaded 'love' marriage, and in any case, as they are responsible for finding the girl a husband, they feel they do not get any assistance in this matter from their college participation.

Certainly these sentiments are still held by many people. The more conservatives fear that too much education will "spoil" a girl. Nonetheless, study towards a bachelor's degree is becoming increasingly acceptable and functional for urban middle class women. Much more concern is expressed by parents regarding the advisability of post-graduate study for females. A graduate wife may be sought by many highly educated men, but a post-graduate is not likely to have enhanced her marketability. In addition, the highly educated woman requires a highly educated bridegroom and dowry requirements for such men are often exhorbitant.

A Brahmin lecturer presents some of the dilemmas well, in the following passage :

> If it is arranged marriage, which is very common in Bangalore, education helps in finding a suitable partner. Many families want a girl with some education. They will want a girl with a bachelor's degree. But then they feel if a girl is highly educated, past B.A., she won't know anything else, about the home. They feel she will be too proud. And if a

girl is highly educated, she will have ideas of her own, and it becomes very difficult. She will naturally want a boy superior to her and unless the family is very well off, it will be difficult to get a suitable partner. When a girl is highly educated and she sees the different boys coming to the house she may not like them.[10]

The number of unmarried females in India has always been small; it is suggested here that highly educated urban women may increasingly fall into this category, especially if they refuse matches unsuitable, from their point of view. In a brief article concerned with the fate of spinsters, I. Bhatnagar (1964 : 19) makes a similar observation :

With the spread of female education women demand a choice in the matter [marriage]. Many of them would rather choose to remain a spinster than lead an unhappy life with a partner who is not up to them. A few of them inflict self-sacrifice on themselves and refuse to be bound in wedlock because they find their parents cannot find a dowry for them or if they can, it will land them in an economic hardship for the lifetime. In middle class families parents in their anxiety to find a suitable match for their daughters wait too long till their girls cross the usual age limit, making their marriage a difficult proposition . . .

Sometimes a woman is compelled to remain virgin to be able to support her family. The parents or relatives who compel a young woman to refrain from marriage for their own self-interest are deserving of censure. The young woman is deeply wronged.

On the other hand, some of these educated women may begin to find their own mates, and even cross caste barriers in doing so.

Any statement about the level of education considered desirable in an Indian wife should be qualified by specifying the caste, religion, education, and economic circumstances of the parties involved. Certainly for some rural Indians, the high school graduate stands handicapped for marriage. For many urban educated men, the college graduate is just about right. And for a few others, the college lecturer or doctor may make up in potential income her possible lack of subservience.

Consciousness of obligation to the broader society

As part of the small educated elite of India, do respondents feel that they have an obligation to others outside the family circle? Or is education seen only as it affects themselves? A loaded question, recognizably so, was asked, "Do you feel that you are expected to contribute to the society in any special ways because of your education?" Table 11 shows the distribution of explanations given by women with different educational aspirations. Teaching and voluntary social service are named most frequently. Only those who have advanced degrees or who hope to acquire them feel that they can contribute in fields of work other than teaching, and they cite this more than one-fifth of the time.

TABLE 11—OPINIONS OF EDUCATED WOMEN AS TO HOW THEY ARE EXPECTED TO CONTRIBUTE TO SOCIETY

Ways in which society expects her to contribute	Total		Those who expect education to end with first degree		Those who aspire to or have advanced degrees	
	No.	%	No.	%	No.	%
In general ways	16	16	5	18	11	15
Teaching	45	45	14	50	31	44
Social service	19	19	7	25	12	17
Household, family, children	4	4	2	8	2	3
Work, other than teaching	16	16			16	22
Total	100	100	28	101	72	101
No special ways	5		2		3	
Don't know	3		2		1	

*Table refers to number of times each way is mentioned. Some individuals gave multiple answers. One respondent was not asked for this information and another did not give educational plans. Thus, 95 respondents are represented in this table.

Another interesting finding is that contribution through one's own household, family or children is mentioned in only 4 per cent of the answers. Although many national leaders have stressed the importance of educating women in order that they become more enlightened mothers and wives, this idea is hardly reflected in these responses. Only 8 per cent of the sample say that they are not expected to contribute to society or don't know whether or not they are. Certainly the answers reflect some sentiment on the part of educated women that they are expected to use their knowledge in vocational fields, even though almost a fifth see the traditional charitable effort in social service as befitting their status.

CHAPTER 4

TRADITION AND CHANGE IN VIEWS OF MARRIAGE

Features of Indian marriage system

INDIAN kinship, marriage and family systems have been a major area of investigation for sociologists and anthropologists. If one considers the many regional, caste, religious and rural-urban differences, the project of simply describing these systems is an enormous one. In addition, concern with the effects of westernization on the traditional joint family is reflected in much research about its variations, strengths, and weaknesses. In contrast, and with a few notable exceptions, studies of women's roles have only recently been accumulating.[1] This is especially true of field research which taps the experiences and attitudes of women directly, through interviews and questionnaires. Much of this literature, such as the present work, was first written in the sixties and seventies. Our findings about urban educated women in various parts of India tend to be in agreement. Thus, despite local variations, certain trends appear to be nation-wide—a conclusion reached also by the Committee on the Status of Women in India in their 1974 report.

The attitudes and behaviour of the women we study can be interpreted within the framework of certain widespread features of the Indian marriage system. New conditions—both economic pressures as well as opportunities—are slowly bringing about changes in some traditional practices. Others are being reinforced.

According to one author, the ideal of arranged marriage is still strong. In an important article summarizing studies of women, Singh (1975 : 214) writes :

One aspect of marriage which cuts across specific systems of kinship and marriage in India . . . is the system of arranged marriages. Arranged marriages are practised by all segments of the society, with the partial exception of portions of the Anglo-Indian community . . .

In 1967, many of our respondents greeted questions about marriage with diffidence, as already noted. The open preoccupation (at that time) of young Western women with dating and mating had ill-prepared the senior author for the professed indifference of Indian women to this major event.[2]   Literature on the formal aspects of arranged marriage did little to suggest that women in their middle twenties would say, "I have not thought about marriage." However, as understanding of the Indian marriage system deepened, the meaning behind this type of response became clear.

Necessary clues appeared as we examined crucial norms and values defining the Indian female's attitude toward marriage.   Some of these have already been discussed : the notion of women's perpetual tutelage and dependence on men, the belief in their extreme sexuality, the idea of individual nature, and the importance of reputation, position and gossip. Here we go on to examine briefly, as context for our findings, a number of other related aspects of Indian life.   These include not only cultural prescriptions, but also modes of relationship within the family.   The following will be considered : the role of fatalism, religion and magic; the compulsory nature of marriage and the issue of dowry; the prescribed duties of fathers and daughters; the nature of family conflict and compromise, and the use of third parties and indirection.

Reliance on fate

Many respondents, but especially the more conservative, profess a reliance on fate.   They may verbalize hopes about continuing their education, but take a much less active stance towards marriage.   The latter is understood as an event which happens, and to which one must "adjust." In the past, this resignation to fate has been appropriate, for marriage was compulsory for women and marital choice the problem of elders. Further, during the time of child-marriage, the young bride could not be expected to look forward to leaving her home to live with strange in-laws.   The bridge between marriage and past roles has always been duty, and the young bride, however unwilling, was expected to accept her fate. The college graduate, who has been out in the world, and who hears and knows more about marriages, is probably less able to keep her mind "blank" about it; yet, culturally, that is the right thing.   The traditional woman may internalize this stance, making it difficult for her to develop a role in marital choice if she is offered one.   This was true of many of the young Japanese studied by Robert Blood (1967 : Chap. 1).   Marriage was considered an inevitable occurrence which required no judgment or intervention on their part.   When these young Japanese were given the right to choose their own mates many did not enjoy exercising it. The young Indian woman today may still hear about parents' activities in searching for a mate for her almost by chance.

The importance of marriage is considered such that, in many cultures, marital choice is not left to the young. Youth themselves may accept the judgment of their elders as superior. Most Indian women do not find their own mates but they have much opportunity to learn about the proper behavior expected of the ideal wife, through stories, epics and anecdotes.

The father does have the awesome duty of selecting life partners for his children, and may depend ultimately on the matching of horoscopes, as well as the advice and help of his wife and other family members. According to Altekar (1962 : 72), the practice of consulting horoscopes came into prominence along with child marriage, thus providing support for the father who had the duty of making fateful decisions for young children. The use of horoscopes was intended to minimize risks, and continues to ease tension for some fathers. For example, one may be told by an astrologer that his daughter is not fated to be married for some time, and hence he need not begin the search for a husband. In contrast however, an otherwise suitable union may be ruled out because the young peoples' horoscopes do not match. The functions and dysfunctions of reliance on horoscopes could profitably be studied.

Prevalence of the dowry system

Marriage had come to be regarded as obligatory for girls by about 300 B.C., according to Altekar (1962 : 32). The norm became so powerful at the beginning of the Christian era that it resulted in various abuses. A daughter with some obvious disability or disease might be married to a highly undesirable person. According to Kapadia (1966 : 137), the high cost of dowry in modern times still leads to unsuitable matches.

Thomas maintains that a "commercial motive" in dowry developed during the later British period. A young man with a good education and good prospects became much sought after as a bridegroom, and parents of girls vied for the available prospects. ". . . [D]owry, in due course, became the deciding factor in the marriage market among several communities in India" (Thomas 1964 : 372).

Since dowry, along with the high cost of marriages, is frequently condemned in print, it is surprising to find that 40 per cent of respondents answer "yes" when asked whether or not dowry is customary in their communities.[3] An approximately equal number maintain that it is not customary and the remainder say the practice varies within their communities.[4] Almost half of the married and engaged women say that it is not given in their communities, and they would be well-informed by their own experience.

The prevalence of dowry may well be underestimated in these figures. Not only does the definition of dowry vary, but it is both illegal (by the Dowry Prohibition Act of 1971) and widely disapproved. There is also public acknowledgement that legal efforts have been minimal and unsuccessful in enforcing this Act.

A number of the husbands of sample members who are most favorably inclined towards their wives' employment did not accept dowry. In 1967, we observed that the economic value of a working wife might become a substitute for dowry. According to varied sources the requirement that a woman be qualified to work is sometimes added to dowry requirements instead. While a group of Mehta's respondents who were strongly opposed to dowry maintained that a good education substituted for it, they came from highly prestigious families who would not expect difficulties in finding bridegrooms (Mehta, 1970 : 133). Occasionally parents would discuss this issue with us, and it was a frequent topic of criticism in academic circles. However, even those most opposed to the custom sometimes had to compromise by giving expensive gifts to the bridegroom and his family and by spending large sums of money on the weddings. The social pressures are such that parents may feel powerless to take a stand against dowry. Mehta's respondents discussed some of the dilemmas involved and their own ambivalences (Mehta, 1970 : 131-134).

Kurian (1961 : 121), however, maintains that there are some advantages from the dowry system :

Dowry payments mean much financial strain, but have some positive aspects. Girls have a chance of getting better partners when dowry is paid. This smacks of commercialism but it is not so bad as it may seem at face-value when we consider the conditions under which they marry. Arranged marriages are still the most prevalent form, and when there is a possibility of choice between two or three eligible girls, the boy might naturally choose one with some financial security as, in the absence of free choice, emotional ties have little meaning for him.

Dowry payment thus helps the girl to make the best match. It also has a useful function when the girl is educated but not good-looking. The attraction of sufficient monetary compensation in the form of a dowry might tip the scale in her favour when the boy is not particular about looks. Dowry thus forms a kind of social security and also makes up for property claims. It is considered desirable for a girl to be married with a substantial sum as dowry, and, in addition to the obvious financial considerations, there are prestige points. Girls who have no dowry are looked down upon by the family of the boy. Sometimes this even affects those who marry for love.

Much of Kurian's reasoning holds up for families which have sufficient wealth to pay the required dowries. The women who have a chance of getting better partners are those whose parents can afford more bountiful dowries.

Even with the dowry system, the strong prescription favoring marriage led to a situation in which there were virtually no unmarried adults in traditional India (Goode, 1963 : 236). The universality of marriage has persisted, despite the distinct tendency towards the rise in age at marriage already noted. According to the 1961 Census, even urban women are almost all married by the time they reach age 34 (India, Ministry of Information and Broadcasting, 1965 : 529). In 1971, 99 per cent of all women in the age group 25-44 are listed as "ever married" (Sinha, 1977).

Career as possible substitute for marriage

The percentage of highly educated urban females is so small that slight changes in their marriage rates would not be reflected in national ones. However, the growing economic independence of women, as well as gradual changes in patterns of mate selection, may affect these rates in the future. Levy (1949) has suggested that higher education enables a girl to become aware of alternatives to marriage.[5] In addition, it will be seen that families are beginning to accept the right of at least some of their daughters to substitute career for marriage. A national report (Government of India, 1974 : 88) claims,

In pre-independence days some women had voluntarily decided against marriage in order to devote their life to the national cause or social service. Today in the professions, services, and in the field of social work, we have a number of successful unmarried women who enjoy high status.

Educated women who rebel against the idea of dowry are beginning to view the possibility of life-time careers. One of the youngest respondents, already studying for her master's degree in a scientific field, spoke most vehemently against arranged marriage, as follows :

The dowry is just like buying something on the market, just like selling goods. I won't go in for arranged marriage, no matter what. I think that if a girl marries her education will be wasted. I am not interested in marriage. I can do more for the country if I am not married.

Arranged marriage remains father's preserve

If it is the father's sacred duty to find a husband for his daughter and to insure continuous male protection for her after his death, what does this imply for the daughter's role ? She is certainly not primed to "fall in love." "Love marriage" is a frequently used concept, but falling in love is considered an accident rather than the active seeking out of a mate. The anxiety of finding husbands is traditionally that of the father. Thus Ross (1961 : 321) can write, with some justification :

It could be argued that Hindu girls have one great advantage over western girls in college in that, as their marriages are still arranged by their parents, they do not have to worry about finding husbands themselves during their college years; whereas girls in western colleges are often faced with two of the most difficult tasks of their lives at the same time—that of finding a husband and preparing themselves for future careers.

What if the young woman is concerned about her marriage or is afraid that it might not come to pass ? To question her father would be indelicate, might intimate that he is not doing his duty, and might reflect interest in sexual matters. The following episode illustrates :

A single Christian woman, 25 years of age, was interviewed by the author and a Christian assistant. Because the respondent's shyness and apparent embarrassment might have been due to the author's presence, two assistants were sent back for further informal conversation. Their encounter with an angry father is described below :

The father told us that the interviewee was much upset because of the interview carried out on her on the 27th. He said the questions on marriage should not be discussed with an unmarried and inexperienced girl as it would spoil her mind and besides that, she would not know anything about marriage. He seemed to be a very religious-minded person and said that we cannot decide anything about marriage, as everything takes place according to God's will. He even quoted certain lines from the Bible. I tried to convince him that whatever we take down will be kept confidential and will not be revealed to anyone. He still insisted that he doesn't mind us asking her anything, but questions on *marriage* should *not* be asked, as he himself knows that her mind is blank on this subject and that she is very innocent and can't answer such questions.

For this daughter to admit that she had thought about marriage would have been a confession of evil thoughts and lack of innocence.

The traditional attitude of the young woman is probably well-expressed by the respondent who, when asked if her future plans included marriage, replied, "That is the father's duty. I can adjust." Marriage has been considered necessary in order for a woman to achieve her highest place and insure her security. Tales of the unfortunate fate of spinster relatives might help a girl to understand this, and prepare her for the inevitable.

"Adjustment"—Woman's duty

"Adjustment," the woman's duty, is used very broadly to refer to any situation in which a woman is placed in a new, different or disagreeable position. Thus, if the parents refuse to allow her to work, she adjusts; if she goes to live with orthodox in-laws, she adjusts to their ways. In doing so, the woman adopts rationalizations which help her to accept her fate. Adjustment also takes the form of a highly developed sensitivity to the needs and wishes of others. The most artful women become masterful at manipulation, learning to wait for the proper time, circumstances and issues on which they can express their own viewpoints. Once married, the young bride is expected to look up to her husband, as lord and master, anticipate his "will and wish" and cater to his needs. Her obligations to her in-laws are very strong, as they have been to elders in her own family. In effect, she practises the same arts of adjustment that she has previously learned, but does not have the advantage of doing so with people very familiar to her.

Open conflict within the Indian family is feared and disapproved; and

youth hesitate to hurt parents or in-laws. One finds the hope that, within
the family, discussion will lead to compromise or to convincing one member of another's position.   Even those who admit to open disagreements
with parents express the wish not to hurt them.   A very outspoken non-
Brahmin Hindu, studying for her M.A., said that she planned to marry
out of her caste if that should be necessary in order to get an educated
mate.   As an afterthought, she added, "Sometimes I think I should try
to please my father because the others [sisters] didn't."   This concern for
parents above oneself was revealed many times.

   Ross' findings are similar.   In her study of student indiscipline, she
tried to ascertain the extent of family disagreement and conflict.   While
most of the college students in her sample disagreed with their parents on
some points, they "did not dare reveal their feelings because they could
not face family displeasure" (Ross, 1969 : 141-142).   Of the 91 women
students in her sample, 32 admitted to quarrelling with mothers but only
14 to quarrels with fathers.   Ross (1969 : 142) concludes :

   Quarrels at home are kept to a minimum in many of the families
   because the children either respect their parents and do not want to
   hurt or challenge them, or have not the courage to express their own
   views.

The partners' role in arranging marriages

   When family discussion develops around an issue on which there is
disagreement, the opinions of various family members may be sought. A
woman with the prestige and self-confidence inspired by a college degree
is more likely than a less-educated daughter to feel bold enough to enter
into such talks with elders.   Thus, we may expect a change in the educated woman's position of influence within the family without necessarily
anticipating the sharp and open conflict characteristic of some other cultures.   Within the in-law family, of course, she will have to respond more
carefully and show that she knows her place.

   Neighbors, relatives, and friends, as well as professional matchmakers
may be involved in arranging marriages.   One of the motivations for the
use of third parties is the opportunity to influence people without their
knowing the ultimate source.   Thus even when the concerned individuals
seem to be passive in their own marriage arrangements, they may be playing a role.   Since third parties can be approached to suggest particular

matches, the percentage of "love marriages" may be higher than is apparent. The use of go-betweens may prove a helpful mechanism in the transition between arranged marriage and the probably increasing number of self-selected mates.

The essentiality of marriage and problems of unmarried women

Seen within the cultural imperatives discussed above, a number of answers to questions about marriage made more sense. Variations in response often reflected an individual's traditionalism. Having made the proper modest show of disinterest in marriage, most women would go on to discuss such questions as the role of education in affecting marital chances and in adjusting to marriage, the proper age at which they thought a woman should marry, and whether or not they believed a girl could live a happy life without marriage. A few of the more traditional were unwilling to elaborate much in their answers; others went on to tell anecdotes about various women of their acquaintance.

In contrast to the others, the nine women who maintained that they did not intend to marry volunteered this information almost as soon as the subject of marriage came up. They took an active stance toward their own fate and often claimed that their will would prevail. These cases will be discussed in greater detail later in the chapter.

Let us look now at some of the views expressed in response to a number of questions about marriage,

To get respondents' viewpoints about the possibility of life without marriage, we asked, "Do you feel that a girl who does not marry can lead a happy life or that she cannot ?"[6] Fewer than half of the 95 responding said that she could not. More than a third were unequivocal in their position that a woman could be happy without marriage, while an additional 17 per cent believed that she could be happy under proper circumstances. Thus, a large proportion of these educated women do not accept the dictum that marriage is essential. Furthermore, in explaining their positions few hold that marriage is a matter of duty. Their reasoning will be explained shortly.

Breaking down the sample by projected educational attainment and marital status produces interesting contrasts (Table 12). Those women who hold advanced degrees are grouped with the ones currently studying for a second or third degree, and are contrasted with the ones who hold one bachelor's degree and are not now studying. About three-fifths of

the first, more educated group maintain that a woman can, or sometimes
can be happy without marriage, while only about two-fifths of the less
educated do so.[7]   However, this difference is not statistically significant,
and the possibility of a relationship needs further study.

TABLE 12—OPINIONS ABOUT A WOMAN'S HAPPINESS WITHOUT
MARRIAGE, BY EDUCATION AND MARITAL STATUS

Status	Can a girl who does not marry lead a happy life ?			
	Total	No	Yes	Sometimes
Projected Education				
Higher degree				
number	55	21	22	12
per cent	100	38	40	22
B.A. or B.Sc.				
number	40	23	13	4
per cent	101	58	33	10
Marital Status				
Single				
number	76	31	31	14
per cent	100	41	41	18
Married				
number	19	14	3	2
per cent	101	74	16	11

Work is only now becoming only a realistic alternative to marriage for
middle class Indian women.   Those who hold advanced or professional
degrees have much better career possibilities than women with bachelor's
degrees.   Even so, women who are highly qualified may have difficulty in
finding suitable work, given a serious unemployment problem (Government of India, 1974 : 220).   Those who do find high status jobs may, in
turn, have raised their standing in the marriage market.

The view that one can be happy without marriage may also represent
anticipatory socialization to the spinster role.   At least *some* individuals

(Bhatnagar, 1964 : 19), an Indian journal very much concerned with advancing the cause of women : ·

> The unmarried woman has emotional needs which have to be satisfied. One of them is the hunger for motherhood. The decision to remain unmarried for life is not good, as a rule, for the mental health of a woman. Love is a woman's whole existence. It dominates a woman's life.

References to criticism and social pressures are made by a surprisingly small proportion of respondents (18 per cent). One woman believes that a girl should marry, if only to prevent her parents from being criticized. But others indicate that the woman herself may not have an easy time. A young mother describes the plight of an unmarried woman in this way : "In the case of a joint family, she is all the time nagged at and she is not left in peace." An unmarried Brahmin claims : "If one is not married, she has to face the rubbish comments from society." While it appears that societal pressures on the unmarried woman are lessening, traditional living arrangements and the needs for protection and companionship still present practical difficulties.

The legitimization of spinsterhood

Those respondents who feel marriage is not essential to happiness demonstrate how the role of spinster is becoming legitimitized. The reason mentioned most frequently, totalling one-quarter of the responses, is that there are satisfactory alternatives to marriage. This not only takes cognizance of new opportunities but also fulfills the past requirement that women be kept busy. Suitable careers as well as social service work are mentioned as ways of doing so. An unmarried Moslem in her late twenties claims that a girl can adjust to being unmarried if she is occupied : "An unmarried girl can lead a happy life provided she is employed, because she will be occupied, independent, and have no time to brood over it." However, a young Brahmin shows a much more positive evaluation of single life : "Yes, a girl who does not marry can lead a happy life. She need not worry about family and all. And she can work more for the country rather than for her own self."

The untraditional viewpoint that an unmarried woman may be independent best illustrates change in role conceptions and is voiced in fully one-fifth of the explanations. The term "independence" usually refers to financial independence, but sometimes also to independence from ties of marriage and family responsibilities, as in the last statement above. Financial independence implies that the woman is no longer dependent on the family for funds, though she may indeed contribute to it. Her economic role will be recognized in increased status within the family, even though her salary may be turned over to the male head of the house. For some women, the independence attached to remaining single means one will not have to cater to the wishes of a husband. As such, it makes explicit the rebellion against existing role definitions.

The notion of independence does not appear to include the premise that independent living arrangements are possible. Respondents who say that a woman need not marry tend to minimize the problems of companionship and security. Few of them mention the need for a proper home environment, so prominent in arguments of women who feel marriage is essential. The bypassing of this issue suggests that living arrangements for the unmarried are not considered ideal even by the group who speak more favorably of single life.[10]

Twenty-one per cent of answers explaining why marriage is not essential refer to the particular qualities or "nature" of the woman. Among qualities spelled out are: having will power, being adjustable, being spiritually-minded, and not "liking marriage" or not being suited to marriage. Will-power enables one to resist sexual temptation or to overcome social disapproval. Adjustability is considered necessary for a home situation in which one never takes on the wife role, and remains subordinate to other females. A woman who has been earning for a long while or who has an engrossing career may be considered less suited to running a household. Here we see that the accepted belief in differences in nature permits some divergence from the rule that girls should be married.

While not all take the position with equal vigor, the nine women who maintain that they will not marry are publicly proclaiming themselves as deviants from cultural expectations. They define their nature as not suited to the marriage role and imply that, as a consequence, the parents' wishes will not predominate. Their confidence that parents will respect their feelings suggests that such an understanding may already exist. By stating openly that they do not wish to marry, these women temper society's speculation that something is wrong with the family or that the father is not fulfilling his duty. This stance differs clearly from that of respondents who claim to have not thought about marriage; the rejection of marriage implies that some thought has been given to the subject.

In some cases it may have been taken for granted that because of an early illness or disability, the woman was not destined for marriage. Her chances for obtaining a desirable bridgeroom may be considered limited. One individual indicated that she had grown up accustomed to the idea that she, among her sisters, would never marry. Another, a nineteen year old, whose family is well off, appeared to be somewhat sickly. She volunteered the following : "I have decided not to marry. My sisters—they will be happy married. [But what if your parents want you to ?] No, they will do as I say. They will agree with me."

During the follow-up study, the authors met with two women who, in 1967, had said they would not marry. One had acquired a Ph.D. and was in a teaching post. Her family recognized her as having an important career and did not demand that she help with home tasks. Single, she entered into decision-making about the marriages of her other sisters. In another case, the woman had been married to a man who was not highly educated, and whose family had been informed about what was considered a minor disability. The fact that she had a permanent government job, a decent income, and was good-looking may have been counterbalancing factors. Despite the assumption on the part of her immediate family that she would not marry, other relatives disagreed, and helped to arrange this match.

An educated woman who is helping to support her family may be well aware that her earnings are needed, as illustrated by the case of a 30-year-old Brahmin. She is described by the interviewer as follows :

She is working because of the financial difficulties. She is still unmarried. As such she doesn't think of marriage at all. She feels very strongly that a girl can be happy without marriage. They do not have to bother. Neither children nor family conflicts. She says that she is not intending to marry . . . She was frank about the family income and told me it is necessary for her to work to balance the family expenditures.

According to various sacred texts, the daughter in a family lacking a male heir might be declared an appointed daughter and take the place of a son in performing religious duties. The marriageability of this substitute son ("Putrika") was sometimes held in question (Shastri, 1959 : 19). Similarly, it seems that a highly educated daughter may now be considered eligible to take the son's place in helping to support parents and younger siblings. Under present circumstances, an employed daughter is no longer able to help her parents once she gets married, but is expected to give her salary to her husband. Hence, her marriage may be postponed indefinitely.

Ross (1961 : 201-202) also refers to this new economic role of middle class women in *The Hindu Family in its Urban Setting*, describing in detail a case in which a young woman gave up the prospect of marriage so that she could help her family financially. The same investigator found the economic role of women to be even more pronounced in her later studies.[11] Of the employed women in our sample, 77 per cent were giving more than half of their earnings to their families.

Five women in the follow-up study (17 per cent of those responding) are unmarried. One is a member of a religious order, as she had been in 1967. Asked to explain reasons for not yet being married, and given seven alternatives, three women ticked off the traditionally acceptable response, "I prefer to stay unmarried." The last woman wrote in : "Engaged to be married to a person of a different caste; self-chosen." She is the most highly educated woman in the sample and her future husband has an equivalent education. They are working at the same place.

Towards Equality (Government of India, 1974 : 85) also comments on the case of the working daughter, as follows :

In some families, the earnings of the girl are set aside for providing her dowry and marriage expenses but gradually, the inhibition of the parents to be supported by the earnings of a daughter is also breaking down. There are extreme cases of parents not wanting the daughter to get married, as it would deprive them of her earnings.

That some women lack enthusiasm for marriage must also be considered in view of Theodorson's findings (1968 : 131) about cross-national variations in eagerness to marry. Comparing Indians, Burmese, and Chinese in Singapore, he points out that in all three cultures motivation to marry was traditionally supported by strong sanctions. Finding what he considers a large percentage of female college students who express a desire not to marry, Theodorson concludes that there has been a decline in the strength of traditional motivations for marriage. Comparing the three cultures, Indian women proved to be the most averse to marriage, with 28 per cent of them answering that they would not like to marry if it were up to them.

In discussing the necessity of marriage, a number of our respondents point out that marriage itself does not insure happiness. A single Brahmin studying for her M.Sc. had this explanation :

An unmarried girl can certainly lead a happy life. Highly qualified girls are sometimes incapable of adjustment. Marriage is not necessary for a happy life. Many marriages are unsatisfactory and independence is preferable to an unhappy marriage.

Others mention such possibilities as early widowhood, forced marriages, difficult husbands, or orthodox in-laws. Thus, the point is made that chances of unhappiness are present in either case, whether one marries or remains single.

Influence of women's education and employment on marital choice

Kurian (1961 : 67), in his study of married Syrian Christians from the State of Kerala, describes four patterns of marital choice, as follows : marriage which is (1) arranged according to the ideas of the parents; (2) arranged by the parents with the consent of the respondent; (3) the respondent's own choice with the consent of the parents; and (4) the respondent's own choice without the consent of the parents. The second pattern was most frequent among both his urban and rural respondents. Members of our sample also consider this pattern most prevalent, but perceptive education as providing the woman more influence. A small proportion see education or employment as enabling a young woman to choose her own mate.

While opinions about the prevailing marriage system were not sought directly, several questions elicited assumptions about it. Among these were the questions of whether education and employment help or hinder a girl in finding a suitable marriage partner.

Respondents often cite the continuing existence of arranged marriage to clarify other answers. For example, a married Moslem states :

I think education helps a girl to find a suitable partner, but here in India 75 per cent of the parents arrange a match, and it is for them to decide what and who is suitable for their daughter.

Remarks referring to the second pattern named by Kurian were more frequent. A single Brahmin maintains, "Employment helps a girl in contact with different men, and she learns what type of man would suit her best. The partners are still chosen by parents, for the girl's inspection."

Respondents were asked how education aids in mate selection. The

reasons given most frequently imply that a degree is an asset in the traditional marriage market. Thus, 46 per cent of the responses hold that some
men or their parents prefer graduates for wives. More than a third of the
responses reflect the belief that the educated woman has increased influence on her parents' selection, with the reason being that education makes
a woman more knowledgeable and more willing to express her opinions
about men. While 9 per cent of the respondents go so far as to suggest
that educated women may select their own mates, they probably would not
condone such action without parental approval. Judging from the tone
of the total interviews, these college-educated women rarely consider acting against the expressed wishes of their parents. The bolder ones persist
longer in attempting to convince parents to accept their viewpoints.

TABLE 13—COMPARISON OF THE EFFECTS OF EDUCATION AND
EMPLOYMENT ON MARITAL CHANCES

	Education		Employment	
	No.	%	No.	%
Helps	60	63	36	39
Hinders	8	8	22	24
Neither; or, sometimes helps, sometimes hinders	27	28	35	38
Total	95	99	93	101

Comparing the assessment of the effects of education and employment,
respectively, on marital chances (Table 13), we see that education is definitely viewed more positively. Sixty-three per cent of respondents say
that education helps in finding a mate, but only 39 per cent feel this is true
of employment.[12] Table 13 shows that over a third of the respondents
believe that the effect of employment on marital chances varies—that it
sometimes helps and sometimes hinders, or that it may do neither. This
viewpoint reflects a changing situation in which employment, once stigmatized for middle class women, is gaining legitimacy. Chapter 5 deals at
length with the question of the respectability of work. Note, though, that
its legitimacy has continued to increase. Asked what changes they had
observed in the last ten years, our follow-up respondents frequently point
to the growing number of employed women. Questionnaire returns, in-

terviews, and the research of others all indicate that more men are seeking working brides, and more families finding them acceptable.

Returning now to our original data, although employment is considered to be less helpful than education in finding a partner, the reasoning again suggests presuppositions about arranged marriage.

TABLE 14—HOW EMPLOYMENT HELPS IN FINDING A PARTNER

		Responses	
		No.	%
1.	Girl can help boy economically	24	38
2.	Girl may choose own partner	11	17
3.	Boys like employed girls	9	14
4.	Some boys' families like employed girls	5	8
5.	Girl has more knowledge of people and desirable traits	5	8
6.	Girl is known and seen by more people	4	6
7.	Girl has more to say in influencing parents' choice	1	2
8.	Other	2	3
9.	Believe it helps but no reason given	3	5
	Total	64	101

Interpreting various explanations (Table 14), one notes that employment may be viewed as an asset in the traditional marriage market or alternatively as providing more opportunity to enter into choice of mate. Thus, the statement, "an employed girl can help her husband economically" means that her value to the prospective family is enhanced. The statement, "she can get to know more people" suggests greater opportunity to use her own judgment. A Brahmin lecturer implies that employed women will make better use of their veto power over the parents' choice. And a Hindu stenographer, of a non-Brahmin community, shows how traditional patterns of mate selection can be modified : "When in employment she can meet people. Some third person who comes to know about this may tell the parents, and it can be arranged thus."

Knowledge about a potential bride, and her availability is of some importance. The working woman will be known and seen by more people. Eleven women say that an employed girl can choose her own partner.

Thus we can observe the nascent belief that education and employment may be used to modify patterns of marital choice, as indeed appears to be happening in some cases.

Furthermore, these explanations illustrate the ways in which the transition from arranged marriage toward marriage by choice may take place. The educated woman feels that she is in a better position to judge the candidates presented by her parents than she would be if she were uneducated. Hence, even before structural facilities are available for individual choice (e.g., an approved dating system), the woman has started to develop criteria relevant for mate selection. At first she may use much the same standards as her elders, as does this lively young Brahmin clerical worker. Only in her last sentence does she indicate any concern with personal qualities :

An uneducated girl knows nothing of the world, will just take whom her parents say, whatever they tell her—'he's a graduate,' 'he is well-settled,' she'll accept. But the educated girl knows much more and can choose better. She knows which degrees are better. I wouldn't want to marry a lawyer, for instance. These fellows have to work very hard. Or a doctor. They have to sacrifice some of their desires. A lawyer will make so much this month, a different amount next month. And a medical practitioner, too. But an engineer, he will make a fixed amount and have fixed hours. If they tell me an Arts graduate, I will know it's not so good as a Science graduate. We will be meeting various boys and seeing how they act, and we can judge.

While educated women claim a potentially greater role in the selection of their mates, their exercise of this option is still to be demonstrated. Some single women may be preparing themselves psychologically to exercise their veto, but there was no case reported where any one had turned down a potential bridegroom. This undoubtedly occurs at times, but its frequency is unknown. A number of married women indicate that they acquiesced readily in their parents' choice, as in the following case :

Education helps the girl to have a frank talk with the future partner and parents. An uneducated girl will not have the courage to go and talk to her parents about her future. In many cases the educated girl can talk. Frankly though, I didn't. My parents would never do anything to harm me, They would look into everything carefully. And so far they have not done wrong by me.

As has already been suggested, the use of third parties provides a bridge toward greater participation in selection by the couples involved. It was indicated that, under the usual system, a woman who is known and seen by many people becomes more prominent as a marital possibility. A young Moslem maintains that "even" among members of her religious group some girls are able to "find husbands through working."[13] She explains that an inquiry about her sister had come through a contact made at the latter's place of employment. In this case, the family happened not to agree to the match. But, in addition, young people may become acquainted with each other at work. Earlier a respondent's remarks were quoted in which she observed that third parties might be utilized to arrange a match desired by the couple involved. While other methods operate informally, the appearance of an arranged marriage is still considered good form. This is implied in the statement of a Christian graduate student, who asserts that some marriages are arranged "in name only."

In 1977, the third pattern described by Kurian appears to be on the increase. Education and employment now bring unmarried men and women together in more acceptable interaction. Friendships may develop. The couple may then seek the aid of others in having a marriage arranged, or approach relatives themselves.[14]

Countervailing trends : the working woman's economic role vs the Sanskritization of dowry practices

The acceptance of an economic role for educated women is reflected in answers which suggest that they may be considered an asset by prospective in-law families. Of those who view employment positively, more than half stress the fact that an employed woman can help her mate financially. Perhaps even more revealing is the fact that the vast majority of respondents believe that a mother may work if her earnings are needed. Almost one-third of our married respondents were working at the time of the interview, while others were seeking work.

The economic role of the potential bride may eventually take the place of dowry. Comparing the reported family practice with regard to dowry of women who are working or seeking work with those who are either at home or studying for higher degrees, we find a significant difference. Those who are employed or seeking employment are much more likely to report that their families do not expect to give or receive dowry (Table 15).[15] A more thorough study of dowry practices might test this correlation.

TABLE 15—DOWRY PRACTICES BY EMPLOYMENT STATUS OF WOMEN

Status	Whether Family Accepts Dowry*							
	Total		Yes		Sometimes		No	
	No.	%	No.	%	No.	%	No.	%
Employed; seeking work	51	54	13	34	9	56	29	73
In school/home	43	46	25	66	7	44	11	28
Total	94	100	38	100	16	100	40	101

* "Accepts dowry" means the family expects to give a dowry.

At present, however, there is general agreement that the practice of dowry has spread. In the short run, women's education has not decreased dowry requirements. Here is one explanation :

An educated girl aspires to marry someone who is better qualified; her parents also have similar aspirations. There is hesitation on the part of young men to marry better educated girls. In fact there is a common expectation in arranged marriage that a boy should be better qualified than a girl. Thus, the more educated the girl is, the more qualified a husband does she need. This necessitates greater dowry. In such situations parents of the girls often feel almost cheated in educating their daughters. Of course, where the girl is allowed to earn and is capable of earning her own dowry, education may be an advantage, but it does not lessen the dowry (Government of India, 1974 : 74-75).

This excerpt continues by suggesting that a married woman's economic contribution in the form of paid work lessens dowry demands :

Only where a girl has taken up a career or has a permanent job will the boy's people be satisfied with a modest dowry (Government of India, 1974 : 75).

It is difficult to ascertain how many families take this position, given the fact that dowry has now spread to communities which did not always practise it. A series of articles in the English language magazine *Eve's Weekly*, entitled "Dowry—the Scourge of Our Time (And All Time ?)" (Veetee, 1978 : 13) describes the modernization of dowry in this way :

Formerly the demand was for money and jewelry. Today the demands have changed and augmented in keeping with the changing society. Besides hard cash, a television set, a refrigerator, a well-furnished flat and a honeymoon abroad are among the demands among the elite, while a wrist watch, a radio set, a cycle, deposit for a room and a suit make up the demands of the labourer.

The adoption of dowry as a symbol of higher status has been described as a case of Sanskritization, whereby members of lower caste groups take on the customs of higher castes. Apparently dowry has increased in villages as well as cities. In her first visit to two Mysore villages in 1955, Epstein observed the widespread practice of bride-price. Females contributed to agricultural labor and were an asset. During her second visit she was surprised to find that bride-price was being replaced by dowry among the wealthier peasants of one village (Epstein, 1973 : 195). The change was explained by the father who pioneered it in terms of both tradition and his current economic position. He withdrew his daughter from agricultural work, then explained that she was no longer an economic asset and required dowry. Further, he wanted a highly-educated bridegroom for this daughter. The final reason he gave was that since Brahmins practised dowry, why shouldn't he ? (Epstein, 1973 : 197). Other caste members followed his lead in adopting the practice.

Here withdrawal from agricultural labor was tied in with dowry, both affording greater prestige for the father. But in another context, its practice tends to increase female employment. First, as has been indicated, parents may allow their daughters to acquire education while waiting for an appropriate marriage to be arranged. This delay gives the family time to arrange for dowry and also provides the young woman with the potential for employment. The unmarried woman may then work to help accumulate her own dowry. As many middle class Brahmins are now allowing their daughters to enter suitable employment (the nature of which will be discussed in Chapter 6), it is quite likely that members of other castes will follow suit.

The role of education in marital adjustment

The area of marital adjustment is one which has recently received much attention, as many educated women attempt to combine work with marriage. In our original study we asked, "What are the major adjustments an educated woman will have to make in marriage ?" For some, the simple response, "She will have to adjust to everything," seems enough. Many answer the question in terms of the group to which the woman will have to adjust.   Twenty per cent mention the need to adjust only to in-laws; 15 per cent only to the husband, and 18 per cent specify the need to adjust both the husband and his family members.   Other modifications of behavior named are : the need to adjust to the customs or environment of the new family, the need to change some aspect of one's personality or ideas, and economic adjustments.   Married respondents tend to be much more specific than the single ones.   A 22-year-old married Brahmin ex-plains her understanding of required behavior as follows :

> She has to intelligently show to the parents-in-law, if it is a joint family, that their way of life suits her, in spite of minor differences . . . Educa-tion helps in the sense that one can have a better understanding of the problems . . . The way my parents brought me up also helped.   They told me to show the family that I like them and that in time I would become one with them.   From education I know that I should not op-pose them on important things.   I will not voice my objections and I will get over it . . . It is much easier to adjust to one person than to the joint family.   I think it is even harder for the man—he has to please his parents and to please his wife.   It's much easier if they are living separately.

A 21-year-old married Christian explains her adjustments thus :

> My husband's family is not very educated.   So with them I have to be simple.   It means not to act like I am more educated than them.   But since I am not living with them, there is no problem to adjust.   Educa-tion helps in making these adjustments. [An educated girl] will be more cultured.   A less educated girl might fight but an educated girl will not like to fight.

Fully 85 per cent of the sample believe that education helps in adjusting to marriage.   Only 5 per cent believe that it hinders, with the remainder saying that education sometimes helps and sometimes hinders.   Over 60 per cent of the reasons given in explanation describe the educated woman as more understanding and more broad-minded. The related reason, that an educated woman will have learned to mix with different kinds of people, received 16 per cent of the mentions.   An equal percentage of answers stress the various types of helpful knowledge that an educated woman can bring to marriage.

Education is viewed as making a woman more rather than less adaptable to her role in the new family. Clearly, respondents feel that education will not cause them to challenge the traditional expectations of obedience to husbands and in-laws, but will enable them to handle role requirements better. In a sense, these young women are describing the expected consequences of culture contact in replacing the past isolation and seclusion of women. The educated woman is pictured as having more understanding, being more knowledgeable, more open-minded, and more "cultured" in dealing with people—provided she is careful not to act self-important because of her education. The respondents imply that past generations of brides have not, in practice, been entirely able to accept their role prescriptions. Despite what she has been taught about adjusting, the uneducated bride finds it difficult to accept the ideas and customs of the new family if these vary from what she has known all her life. Furthermore, because of a lack of social contact outside the family, she is ill at ease and less graceful in relating to her new family.

The few women who feel that education neither helps nor hinders marital adjustment stress the individual qualities of the bride, as exemplified in this statement by a married non-Brahmin Hindu :

She cannot behave as she likes after marriage. Education in the broad sense helps to make adjustments. Sometimes uneducated people can adjust better than the educated. It is not graduation that helps or hinders, but the understanding or the sense of judging what is right and wrong.

The dilemmas of the modern educated woman in adjusting to the traditional wifely role are recognized, but the notion of obedience is not rejected in this thoughtful response, written by a woman now studying for an advanced degree in another city :

Educated women are old enough to have decided opinions. She will have to adjust herself to the husband deciding for her. . . . Education is primarily a hindrance. But, if given second place in her life it is bound to be a help since it cultivates her mind and she will pass on the message of education. . . . Many men expect their wives to help in bringing additional income to the family. But they never help her in the household work. It is impossible for a girl to manage both single-handedly. In effect, she will have to strike a bargain of mutual help with him. When an educated girl of modern outlook is married into a family following old traditions, the problem of adjustment is severe. She finds it hard to keep her independent spirit under control and remember that her husband's word is law. Though education becomes the main reason for the appearance of problems, it again helps in finding an answer to the problems.

One of the problems alluded to is the double burden of the woman who works and yet is expected to handle all household tasks. The majority of women interviewed in 1967 were as yet unmarried and could only anticipate future adjustments. They were eager to work and not familiar with the simultaneous demands of home and work roles.

A few respondents assert that an educated woman is able to modify the traditional role of wife. While this young Christian woman, studying for a second degree, maintains that education helps in adjustment, her explanation is deviant in that it stresses a more independent posture : "The educated girl knows how to behave but she has some independence of mind. She doesn't have to be a doormat. She can think for herself and doesn't have to agree to everything."

Even though it is claimed that an educated woman will be able to adjust well to the usual role of wife, she may not have to play this role in exactly the traditional way. The in-laws may be unable to ignore her education so easily. They may come to share the pride that many parents take in their highly-educated daughters, and accord the educated daughter-in-law a somewhat higher family status. One should also note that some of the expectations voiced by single women are not based on real experience, but on their idealized conceptions of the wifely role.

Expectations of the unmarried women tend to include the prospect of going to live in a joint family, but chances appear more than even that those who marry will eventually be in their own households. Thirteen of the 19 married respondents are now living in nuclear households. To many respondents, the problem of adjusting to a husband seems relatively miniscule compared to the adjustments required in an in-law joint family. However, one may hypothesize that as the nuclear family becomes more common, husband-wife role expectations will undergo some revision. In the process this relationship is likely to become more closely scrutinized and possibly redefined.

Respondent's preferred and actual age at marriage

The trend of preference for later age at marriage, noted by other observers, is confirmed by our data.

In answer to the question, "At what age do you think a girl should get married?" the median approved range is from 21 to 24 years of age. The most frequently chosen lower and upper limits are 20 and 25.[16] Thirteen per cent of respondents suggest a preferred upper limit over age 25, indicating that the acceptable age for marriage may be extended even further. Of the ten respondents who are over 25 years of age, seven are still unmarried.

Married women differ from single ones on the issue of the appropriate age at marriage. Their median preferred range is from 20 to 21 while that of single women is from 21 to 24. The more highly educated respondents envision a wider age range than do the less educated, suggesting average limits of 20 to 24 as contrasted with 21 to 23 by the latter.

The age of each of the single women was compared with the range that she considered suitable for marriage. Of the 76 single women who answered this question, 35 per cent had not reached their preferred minimum, 47 per cent were within the preferred range, and 17 per cent were past the age they considered best for marriage (percentages rounded). It is interesting to note that this last percentage, based on their own views, is considerably larger than the 10 per cent who are past the modal upper limit of 25 years of age.

In the follow-up study, we again asked the women what they consider the appropriate age for marriage, and this was compared with their actual ages at marriage. Both median and mean of the latter are 24. Thus, the largest number, excluding those still single, were married by the top limit of the age range they originally considered ideal.

However, ten years later the median approved range given by both married and unmarried respondents has narrowed to between 22 and 23 years of age; this figure does not change if the answers of the unmarried are subtracted from the total.

Consistent with the above, only 13 per cent of those married consider their age at marriage to have been the most desirable one. Fifty-eight per cent think that a lower age, and 13 per cent that a higher age, would have been preferable.[17] Interviews would be needed in order to probe the meaning of these responses. They do suggest, however, that although a trend toward later marriage has occurred, the extent of the change is not necessarily considered good. Whether this is due to persisting belief in early marriage, personal experiences in the matrimonial state, or other reasons

is not known.   In a study done in Chandigarh, mothers were asked why
they had married their daughters at ages other than those they themselves
thought best.   The availability of suitable marriage partners, dowry, and
other economic factors—actual conditions—determined their actions
(Singh, 1974).

One of the consequences of higher education and later age at marriage
is a reduction of the birth rate.   The median number of children our
married respondents have is two, and only one woman now has more than
three of them.   The vast majority are not planning to have additional
children; none wish to enlarge their families to more than three.

Much has been written recently about the problems of working mothers,
in India and elsewhere.   Some respondents commented about this issue;
others wrote that they were unable to work because of the lack of adequate
child care, the posting of their husbands to jobs where they themselves
could not find employment, and the difficulty in combining work and home
roles.   This subject is one to which we shall return after considering the
general question of female employment.

Chapter 5

WORK : A NEW VALUE FOR DAUGHTERS
OF THE MIDDLE CLASS

Education as a link to employment

INITIALLY education is used to fill a gap of time before marriage and to help insure a match with a highly educated male. Another consequence follows once a woman has been educated : the possibility of her entrance into gainful employment. In 1967, it was a dilemma for middle class families to decide whether or not to allow their highly educated daughters to work. Families faced with a rising cost of living and dowry problems weighed the financial gains from their daughter's income against traditional norms of female seclusion. The effect of employment on the daughter's reputation, the possibility that she would "mix" with men, and their consequences for her marital prospects had to be considered.

This case study shows the processes of decision-making that occur—what goes on in individual families and specific lives—as broad national patterns emerge. By 1977, several books had been written on middle class working women and their problems.[1] It was widely acknowledged that employment had become far more common for members of this group, and that some men were seeking "working brides." Interest now focused on the role overload and role conflicts experienced by working mothers. In the latter part of this chapter we shall return to this issue.

New opportunities for the urban educated woman occur within an economic context that differs widely for various segments of the female population. Development, and accompanying governmental policies, create some jobs for the educated but affect others adversely. The vast majority of Indian women are employed in agriculture, where technological developments frequently displace them.[2] Too, families which prosper economically, tend to withdraw their females from agricultural labor, as a means of enhancing social status (Srinivas, 1977). In industry men tend to be taught the new techniques, again resulting in the displacement of women or in increased wage differentials between male and female jobs (Government of India, 1974; Boserup, 1970).

Towards Equality summarizes what has happened in India generally :

The long term trend in economic participation of women indicates an overall decline both in the percentage of workers to total female population and in their percentage to the total labor force after 1921 (Government of India, 1974 : 152).

However, slight gains are reported for women in certain fields :

According to census occupational categories, there has been a marginal increase in the proportion of women in white collared occupations, e.g. doctors, nurses and other health personnel, teachers, office workers, etc. (Government of India, 1974 : 153).

The ratio of women to men employees in the public sector showed a steady increase in the seventies, although it was still less than 10 per cent that of men (Government of India, 1974 : 185). It is primarily in these white collar and government jobs that urban educated women find opportunities for employment.

A small number of rural women are also gaining higher education. However, the likelihood is that they will have to migrate to urban areas in order to find jobs. A pilot interview study of 12 women post-graduate students enrolled at a rural institute in Tamil Nadu was done by the junior author in 1978. University status had recently been conferred on the institute under study; the women would receive Master's degrees. Parents had sent these daughters for higher education because rural males were now more educated and some were seeking educated wives. Dowry problems were causing some delay in the arrangement of matches. Thus, similar processes appeared to be occurring as were found in our urban sample. Almost all of these highly educated rural women hoped to work after graduation in white collar jobs, and they anticipated that they would migrate to nearby cities in order to find them.

Economic pressures lessen opposition to the employment of women

The respectability of female employment, provided it be "suitable," has increased over the past two decades. As recently as 1955, public opinion polls in India reflected widespread opposition to the idea of female family members working. Referring to these, Goode states :

Public opinion is . . . clearly against the idea of women working. In the November 1955 Public Opinion Survey, 24 per cent of the respondents were in favor of a married daughter taking a job; but only 15 per cent of mothers in the sample approved it. Even among the sample's young and better-educated strata, only 28 per cent were in favor . . . In October of the same year, 70 per cent of the Delhi sample said they would not allow a young unmarried daughter or sister to go out and work. As in most other areas of family opinion, the West Bengali and Calcutta respondents are more liberal : 46.5 per cent of the rural and 49 per cent of the urban West Bengali were opposed, and only 33 per cent of the Calcutta respondents were so opposed. Although the differences are great, widespread opposition is evident (Goode, 1963 : 269).

Although South India is generally considered more conservative than some of the other cities mentioned, Ross (1961 : 201) found that two-thirds of the 62 men in her Bangalore sample were in favor of women "having a career." Her study contains more recent opinion information than most of those cited by Goode. However, Goode has suggested that because Ross' question was asked in a general way, rather than referring to female members of the respondent's own family, a greater number of positive answers may have been obtained. Ross found the women in her sample to be more conservative than men, pointing out that :

. . . less than a third of the seventy-one women replying were favourable to the idea (of careers for women) although about 50 per cent more thought women should have careers in certain circumstances (1961 : 201).[3]

In her later study of female college students, the same author found that "only a small proportion of the students were themselves seriously interested in careers" (Ross, 1969 : 181). While two-thirds of the 91 women included said that they wanted to study for higher degrees, Ross dismisses these answers as being given without serious thought. Regarding their future employment, she adds, "It is one thing for a student to say that she would like to work after she graduates, and quite another matter for her to do so" (Ross, 1969 : 187). This is correct because working is not her own free choice, but a matter of family decision-making.

Nevertheless, Ross, along with others, suggests that economic reasons push the educated woman into work. At the time of her first study, the economic pressures in Mysore State were not considered as severe as those in some other parts of India. In quoting the 1951 *Census of Mysore State* on this question, she suggests that economic problems may provide the impetus for women to enter the labor market ;

The actual number of women holding remunerative jobs is low in Mysore State compared with the rest of India. The *Census of Mysore*
states that the main reason for this is that the pressure for a higher
standard of living has not yet been felt in the state to the extent it has
in provinces containing more and larger cities. In large cities many of
the middle-and-upper class families will have to live in small, expensive
apartments. This will give the women more leisure time for jobs outside the home and will also put more pressure on them to add to the
family income. Indeed, the main reason that so many married Hindu
middle-class women work without reproach is because everyone under-
stands the economic problems of the middle class, and that a wife's
income is often essential to the family's standard of living (Ross,
1961 : 198).

The *Mysore Population Study*, a carefully done sample survey jointly
sponsored by the United Nations and the Government of India (United
Nations, 1961), also claims that few middle-class women were working in
Bangalore in 1951-52, the time of the study.[4] It states :

A large share of the Bangalore labour force is engaged in personal services and related occupations, amounting to 13 per cent of the males
and 33 per cent of the females. This situation is indicative of an insu-
fficient opportunity for employment in more remunerative and more
attractive jobs. .... The concentration of the female labour force in
such occupations, together with the small numbers of women in clerical, sales, and similar jobs, implies that on the whole the employment
of women of higher social and economic status is not customary in
Bangalore to nearly so great an extent as in the cities of economically
more advanced countries. Apparently those women who work in Bangalore come chiefly from low-income families, and they are presumably
compelled to work by economic necessity.

Bangalore's rate of female employment

More recent information indicates that Bangalore ranks high among
other cities of over one million population in the proportion of women in
its working force. In 1971, 8.2 per cent of Bangalore's female population
was in the working force, second only to greater Bombay, a much more
populous city. Because of differing census definitions in 1961 and 1971,
the exact rates of female work participation over the decade are difficult to

compare. States may be compared, since the same definitions were used for all. Karnataka (Mysore) ranked higher among them in 1971 than in 1961 in percentage of urban female workers to total population. Its rank among the states in percentage of rural female workers to total population went down slightly, but was still above the national average (Government of India, 1974 : 156).

Availability of job opportunities

Goode, in his excellent theoretical analysis, repeatedly points to the structure of opportunities, as well as attitudes, as factors affecting women's employment. Thus, for example, he shows that the percentage of female workers in factories dropped between 1950 and 1956, during a period of male under-employment. And writing of India in 1963, he could maintain :

. . . the opposition to a woman entering paid work is great, but at present her opportunities are few and ill-paid. The cost in social standing is not adequately compensated for by the small income, or the greater richness of her life. Moreover, since marriage still occurs at a relatively young age, if the educated girl attempts to establish a genuine career, she may miss her only chance at marriage (Goode, 1963 : 269).

Our data suggest that both opportunities and sentiments have changed. Given current conditions, the movement of the educated woman into the world of work becomes an obvious transition from college or post-graduate studies. Regarding increased opportunities, Ross notes :

The trend toward women working outside the home in India has been accelerated by the new job opportunities opened up by industrialization, particularly in the white-collar categories of employment. The Five Year Plans of the Indian Government have also publicized the growing need for trained and professional workers in many fields, and this certainty of work has probably encouraged many women to train for these occupations (Ross, 1969 : 187).

The need for trained women to serve more traditionally-oriented ones in fields such as health, education, and welfare, helps to foster their employment. Thus, for example, the Education Commission Report of 1965 suggested that special provisions be made to entice woman teachers to

TABLE 16– DISTRIBUTION OF RESPONDENTS BY RELIGION AND
CASTE BY CURRENT EMPLOYMENT AND EDUCATIONAL
ACTIVITY

(in percent)*

Current Activity	All Respondents	Hindu			Non-Hindu	
		Total Hindu	Brahmin	Other Hindu	Moslem	Christian
Studying	30	30	29	32	11	40
Employed	44	45	45	45	44	40
Unemployed						
Seeking job	9	8	8	9	33	0
Not seeking job	14	16	18	14	11	7
Other	2	0	0	0	0	13
Number (100%)	(97)	(73)	(51)	(22)	(9)	(15)

*Percentages are rounded and thus do not total 100%.

(a) Seven of the Moslem women have already obtained a second degree, which helps explain the small percentage now attending school.

(b) One respondent is a member of Catholic order. Another is the daughter of a Protestant minister who considers her unpaid religious and welfare work a "calling."

follow-up study : fewer Brahmins are working.[8]

Returning to the original study, nine of those not employed nor in school are seeking employment. The remaining 14 in this group are being "kept busy" at home. They are probably well-represented by the statement of this 20-year-old, single Brahmin B.A. :

I would like to work but my mother is dead against. . . . For us there is no need to work. In our family, none of the girls is in service. Mother thinks that it is below their dignity if they send their daughters to work. . . . We tried our best to convince our mother. When it did not work out, we are trying to find happiness in the house itself.

Comparing the income and class identification of the 14 at home with the rest of the sample one finds that they appear to come from a somewhat higher income level and class status, on the average.[9] Half of those staying at home had family incomes of 800 rupees a month or more, as

contrasted with a third of the total. As will be seen later, family attitudes appear to significantly affect the decision to stay at home. Twelve
of the 14 "stay-at-homes" have at least one important family member
who does not want her to work. More than half of them are married,
even though married women constitute only 20 per cent of the sample.
In the follow-up, family income is not significantly related to employment status.[10]

How is employment related to educational attainment? Acquisition of
a second degree appears to signify intention to work. We suggested in
Chapter 3 that parents who do not want their daughter to work may
prevent her from studying past the first bachelor's degree. A married
non-Brahmin Hindu explains why she is not allowed to study for a
master's degree: "I like to study zoology M.Sc., but my husband's
people and husband will not allow, since I will not be allowed to work
outside. Hence my education will be of no use."[11]

TABLE 17—DISTRIBUTION OF RESPONDENTS BY EDUCATIONAL
LEVELS BY CURRENT EMPLOYMENT AND EDUCATIONAL
ACTIVITY

(in percent)*

Current Activity	Highest Degree Held	
	B.A.; B.Sc.	Higher[a]
Studying	39	7
Employed	32	75
Not employed		
Seeking work	9	11
Not seeking work	19	4
Doing unpaid religious work	1	4
Number (100%)	(69)	(28)

*Percentages are rounded and thus do not total 100%.
[a]Higher degrees include : Bachelor of Education and Bachelor of Law, for which a
prior bachelor's degree is required; Master of Arts and Master of Science; and the
M.B.B.S., a medical degree.

Looking at Table 17, it can be seen that of the 28 women holding
higher degrees, three-quarters are working and most of the others are

either seeking work or studying for Ph.D.'s. One young woman is a nun and only one other is simply staying at home. This contrasts with 19 per cent of those holding only one degree who are at home.

The relationship between degree of education and employment appears to persist for the follow-up respondents. Sixty-five per cent of those who hold a degree higher than the initial bachelor's are working, compared to 25 per cent of the less-educated women.[12]

Analysis of respondent's and her family's attitudes toward work

In our original study, we asked a number of questions about the women's own attitudes toward work and those of their family members. Here we discuss some of those attitudes.

The vast majority of respondents positively evaluate employment in preference to staying at home. Asked whether or not they would prefer to work if there were no financial need, 85 per cent respond affirmatively. Over 70 per cent of those at home and not seeking employment are willing to express dissatisfaction with their current status and state that they would prefer to work. If those seeking employment are included with this group, the percentage rises slightly. In proportion to their representation in the sample, the preference for work is about the same for married and single women.

While working has acquired sufficient legitimacy for "stay at homes" to verbalize a position contrary to that of family members, acting against the expressed wishes of the family has not. The number admitting to a preference for work probably represents a minimal figure, since the most dutiful women claim that their desires are guided by the wishes of their parents or husbands.

Fourteen women said they would prefer not to work if there were no financial need. Comparison of this group with the 14 who are actually at home is of interest. There is an overlap of four cases between them representing those whose preference to stay at home coincides with their actual situation. Of those who would prefer *not* to work, five are employed, two are seeking work, three are studying, and four are actually at home. Those who are still studying have not had to confront the decision of whether or not to work, and possibly some may marry before it is imminent. But for 18 per cent of the respondents there is an expressed discrepancy between what they would like to do and what they are doing.

Economic need as well as family attitudes appear to be operating in the situation.

This strong preference of respondents for work contrasts with reported attitudes of women elsewhere in the world.   In several western nations, a substantial proportion of both men and women prefer that women stay at home and not follow an occupation.   The highest proportion of women saying they would like to work, even if they did not have to, occurred in a Detroit sample of women already in the labor force.   Sixty-six per cent said they would work even if they did not have to, but more than half gave "noncareer" reasons—such as escape from the household (Goode, 1963 : 63-64).   However, these studies include other than college-educated women.

Studying the participation of American women in the labor force, Oppenheimer (1976 : 15) notes a distinct change beginning in the 1950's and accelerating in the 1960's. That is the increasing tendency for married women to enter or reenter the labor force.   Interestingly enough, attitudes about this behavior were still fairly negative.   Only 34 per cent of the American husbands surveyed by the Michigan Survey Research Center in 1960 definitely approved of married women working (Oppenheimer, 1976 : 46).   The American women's movement of the 1960's and 1970's has had, as one of its major thrusts, the right of women to have independent careers.

Goode (1963) hypothesizes that women are willing to seize new career opportunities where they have been in a socially and economically under-privileged position, and where men are unable to provide for them at an economic level viewed as adequate.   He considers this to be a question of whether women have more to lose or to gain by working.   Certainly from a short-run perspective, members of our sample do not perceive the disadvantages to be greater than the advantages.   Work provides a conti-nuation of the freedom of college days, and earning money a source of respect. Furthermore, the weighing of possible disadvantages to their future is left to parents, the persons most concerned with the problems of marital choice.

Others have suggested that it is misleading to estimate a women's in-terest in work in terms of a "career."   Since studies show that many men are not career-oriented, it should not surprise us to find that many women do not see work from that perspective.   As in the researches quoted by Goode, members of our sample explain their preference for work in terms other than its intrinsic value : "to keep busy" was mentioned most often as a reason, receiving 37 per cent of the responses. A single Brahmin studying for her master's degree explains what "keeping busy" means to her : "I would prefer to work because it would mean that my time is usefully spent. It would keep me occupied and prevent me from falling into bad ways and having bad ideas." Her reasoning suggests that this young woman has accepted parental values about keeping busy : a traditional value is used to help justify a new behavior pattern.

Despite the efforts of their families to keep them busy with correspondence courses, music lessons, needlework, or other arts, those at home frequently feel "bored." The lack of activity because they are not free to travel about, and the absence of telephones in all but the wealthiest of homes, breeds a sense of isolation. For those who are married and away from their own family members, this may be doubly so. For single women sitting at home and waiting to be married, life becomes tedious.

"To make use of my education," receives 19 per cent of the responses explaining desire to work. The comment that education should not be wasted emerges in many contexts and, as a widely accepted value, may be used in argument by young women whose parents doubt the propriety of work. "Should not be wasted" is a term which includes economic connotations, since particular degrees will have value in the employment market.

However, a growing value among young women, the desire for economic independence, is represented by 13 per cent of the responses. Another 12 per cent express the desire to provide service to others. While an elite group of women have demonstrated such interest through volunteer activities in the past, the notion that one can contribute through paid positions is relatively new. It suggests the development of interests outside the family, and some allegiance to the broader society among some middle class women.[13]

The enrichment of knowledge or experience is given as another reason for working. Many women maintain that work as well as college provides opportunities to meet different kinds of people and to widen their horizons. Only 6 per cent of the respondents indicate that work is desired because of interest in a particular field or enjoyment of work itself.

Some respondents suggest that their own positive evaluation of work is not shared by other graduates, and that the dignity of work for women is still held in question. A 22-year-old Brahmin B.Sc. added these comments at the end of the interview :

Further, I would like to add that most of the graduate women have a problem like whether to have their education be useful to others or not, and whether to mix with the uneducated persons, to help them as far as possible, to give them some knowledge about their society; and if they are poor, how to supplement their family income, etc. Some will feel that it is a great loss of dignity for them if they work, as some will think that only poor people will work.

And another Brahmin now studying for her Bachelor of Education degree at an institution outside of Bangalore, wrote as follows :

The main problem of a lady graduate is what to do next. The jobs available are not suitable and so many idle away their time till a husband comes along.... Another problem is the fact that many educated girls scorn jobs because they feel they are too lowly in nature and acceptance of them will result in a loss of status. Girls should be taught the dignity of labour, which should be emphasized in college. This will prevent the waste of so much talent and education.

These status considerations affect not only the decision to work but also the determination of whether or not particular jobs are accepted.

Further education a strong aspiration

The question discussed above offers respondents the choice between working and staying at home. The general question, "If you could do anything you wanted to in the next two years, what would you do ?" brought out an even stronger preference for education. Forty-one per cent of the sample indicate that they would like to engage in further studies. This includes both individuals studying for advanced degrees as well as some of those who already have such degrees. Unquestionably, graduate study is a highly desirable and liberating activity for these young women, already in the very upmost strata of the population as far as education is concerned. College is a happy interlude that precedes and postpones the taking on of responsibilities and adjustments.

Table 18 shows that almost one-fifth of the respondents hope to get a job in the next two years. Other desired activities include changing jobs or continuing in the same one, foreign travel, finishing studies already begun and getting married. Only 7 per cent choose marriage as their immediate aspiration. Many of these preferences appear to be tied to the activity in which the respondent is now engaged. Foreign travel need not be considered an extremely remote possibility, since a number of educated Indians do go abroad. Two women in our sample had come to the United States with their husbands. Looking at the choices by age, class, educational level, and income, we find no particular patterning.

TABLE 18—PERCENTAGE DISTRIBUTION OF ACTIVITIES DESIRED BY RESPONDENTS IN THE NEXT TWO YEARS

Activity	Per cent
Take up further studies	41
Get a job	18
Travel	9
Get married	7
Finish studies	6
Change job	5
Stay in same job	3
Miscellaneous	4
Don't know; no special desire	6
Number	(97)

Caution should be exercised in interpreting these responses, which reflect cultural norms as well as personal feelings. The presupposition of freedom of choice is not easy for respondents to make. A strong feeling of fatalism shows itself in such initial answers as, "That is in the hands of God." As discussed in Chapter 4, reticence to display interest in one's own potential marriage is culturally defined for the Indian woman. Marriage is probably under-represented as a goal, while the desire for education is secular and acceptable enough to be stated openly.

And, of course, the Indian woman knows that her future course does not depend on her own preferences. A father characteristically "puts" his daughter into some academic field or "sends" his daughter into employment. It has already been suggested that the woman's role in determining her own future varies, and is partly dependent first, on her willingness to express her views and then on the strength of her persuasive powers in "convincing" parents of a particular viewpoint.

Economic role of working women

Before looking at the reported attitudes of the family members about employment, a few facts about the economic role of these women should be considered.

If financial considerations are involved in their permitting or advising a young woman to work, the family may be expected to reap some benefits. Our data suggests that this is so, and that the economic duties of the sons of the family are now shared by some of these educated daughters.[14]

Over three-quarters of the working respondents contribute more than half of their salary to the family. Besides the full-time workers, three women studying for advanced degrees are doing "tuitions" (tutoring). Of the two about whom we have information, one surrenders her entire earnings to the family while the other gives nothing. However, in both cases, they assist their families financially. The individual who keeps her earnings pays for all her own expenses, including clothing and gifts.

The follow-up respondents who work were asked the same questions about their family contribution. An even larger proportion—86 per cent—contribute more than half of their salary to the family. Their new role, as paid workers outside the home, may be seen as a way in which women again demonstrate their traditional devotion to their husbands and families. But the data also highlight women's economic part in maintaining living standards.

In the original study, we asked about the pattern of handling salaries. Three patterns are found : the most traditional, in which the whole salary is given to the head of the family and money requested as needed; an intermediate one in which the salary is turned in but a specific allowance returned; and the most innovative, in which the employed woman keeps her whole salary and handles many of her own expenses. The intermediate pattern appears to predominate. Ten women receive money as needed; 29 receive specified allowances, and only four keep their salaries. The most frequent amount of allowance is between 21 and 50 rupees monthly.

Cormack (1961 : 52) reports on dissatisfaction among Indian students with the procedure of having to request money rather than receiving a set allowance. Future studies of working women might include consideration of these patterns and their possible correlation with changing styles of family life. In her studies of working women, Kapur (1974 : 278) describes frictions over how family income is to be spent as one of the elements in marital disharmony.

Family attitudes about respondents' employment

While eight of the working respondents maintain that it is their own idea to work, or that no one has influenced them to do so, the other 35 name one or more relatives as influential. Members of the sample appear to have clearly defined notions about how various members of the family feel about their working. It is obviously a topic which has been discussed in the family.

The father, alone and in combination with other family members, is mentioned by 37 per cent of the respondents as the relative who has had most influence about his daughter's employment. Mother, brothers, and sisters follow in that order. However, from answers to another question, it is clear that had we asked the women staying at home, who had influenced them *not* to work, husbands and parents-in-law would have found significant representation.

The continuing influence of the father in the life of his unmarried daughters was demonstrated in many ways during the interviews. Regardless of how many family members enter into decision-making within the family, the father's formal role is clear. He carries the main responsibility and duty of protecting his daughters and assuring their future.[15] If there is a question about the young woman's education, and inquiries must be made, he is the appropriate person who visits the authorities. In contacts with the world outside the family, he acts for them. This does not mean that the father always plays the dominant role in the all decision-making. However, in both the areas of education and work he is likely to be far more knowledgeable than his usually less well-educated and more isolated spouse. One well-educated father we knew told us that he hoped to put his daughter into post-graduate studies but expected some opposition from his wife.

Each respondent was asked how the following members of her family felt about her working; father, mother, eldest brother (brother 1), next eldest brother (brother 2), third eldest brother (brother 3), sisters as a group, husband or fiance where relevant; and "other" relatives who affect decision-making within her family. If the respondent was not employed, she was asked how family members would feel about her seeking employment. Most women answered readily, differentiating between the views of significant family members, such as two or three elder brothers.[16] A five point scale of statements was given, ranging from "strongly encourages" her to work to "prefers me to stay at home," with the middle category suggesting neutrality or permissiveness. In some of the discussion that follows the first two and last two statements, respectively, are combined, making a three point scale.

As other influential relatives, ten respondents name parents-in-law, while 29 name such relatives as uncles, aunts, grandparents and brothers-in-law. Among this group, uncles are mentioned most frequently. In the majority of cases, the immediate family, parents-in-law, and the respondent herself are most involved in decision-making about work.

Now let us look at the most significant reference figures for our respondents (Table 19). The largest number of each type of family member encourages the young woman to work, rather than taking a neutral position or preferring that she remain at home. It is of interest that in-laws are said to hold a more negative viewpoint than members of the family of orientation. Half of the in-laws whose opinions are known prefer that the daughter-in-law stay at home. Such opinions need not be associated with the in-law role, but may reflect a greater conservatism on the part of the husband's family. For example, the parents-in-law may not permit their own daughters to work. On the other hand, keeping her at home may be considered a necessary way of socializing the daughter-in-law into her new family role.

The strongest encouragement comes from the woman's sisters, with 69 per cent of them favoring her employment. Almost none are reported as preferring that she remain at home. Their sisters' concurrence demonstrates that the appeal of work is shared by many young women besides those in our sample. More than two-fifths of the fathers and mothers also encourage the respondents to work. The last is a surprising figure, considering the conservatism generally attributed to Indian mothers. It is rather unlikely that mothers would encourage behavior considered detrimental to their daughters' futures. A plausible conclusion is not that mothers are becoming less conservative or less interested in their daughters, but that proscriptions against work have become much weaker. Nor are mothers simply agreeing with their husbands, as will be seen when we turn to family agreement and disagreement. More than half of the eldest brothers but less than ten per cent of the third eldest brothers want the respondent to work. The latter group also tends to be less neutral than other

TABLE 19—REPORTED ATTITUDES OF FAMILY MEMBERS ABOUT RESPONDENT'S WORKING

Family Members' Reported Attitude	Father No.	%	Mother No.	%	Brother 1 No.	%	Brother 2 No.	%	Brother 3 No.	%	Sisters No.	%	Husband No.	%	In-Laws No.	%
Total	77	100	86	100	57	100	36	100	18	100	65	100	20	100	10	100
Encourages her to work	33	43	39	45	31	54	17	47	7	39	45	69	10	50	3	30
Neutral	30	39	29	34	20	35	14	39	6	33	17	26	5	25	2	20
Prefers her to stay at home	11	14	16	19	5	9	5	14	5	28	1	2	5	25	5	50
Other	3	4	2	2	1	2	0	0	0	0	2	3	0	0	0	0

(a) One future husband of an engaged woman is included.
(b) Totals represent living family members who are considered as having influence by the respondent. Eight married women gave no information on in-laws.
(c) Other represents opinions which could not be classified according to the scale.

relatives, and we find more than one-quarter of them preferring their sister to stay at home.   More would have to be known about the effect of size of family and relationships of brothers and sisters in order to interpret this rather interesting finding.[17]

Fifty per cent of the husbands encourage their wives to work, while a quarter want them to remain at home.   All family opinions refer to the respondent in her current marital status, yet the percentage of husbands wanting their wives to remain at home is larger than that of any of her other relatives, except the third brother and the husband's own parents. The husbands' attitudes are more conservative than those of their wives' fathers, but are unusually permissive when compared to those of Indian males questioned in previous surveys (Goode, 1963 : 261).

The fact that so many husbands encourage their wives to work suggests the beginning of a pattern in which educated wives may be expected to help out financially in the early stages of marriage, much as they do in other societies.   Whether or not a working wife will play her traditionally sub-servient role is a question that has been raised in other contexts.   Some doubt may be raised also about her willingness to go back to the confines of home after a period of work, and about the family's ability to withstand loss of her earnings.   The hypothesis was suggested that many of these educated women would continue to work throughout the course of their married years.

It is now possible to compare the estimated opinions of relatives of women "at home" with the rest of the sample. A significantly higher pro-portion of fathers, mothers and husbands of those at home prefer that women not work, as seen in Table 20.

Mothers again prove to be less neutral than fathers, with fewer taking the middle, or permissive, position.   More than half prefer the daughter to stay at home, and only two of the 14 actually encourage her to work. Eight of the women at home are married and one is to be married soon; none of the husbands or future husbands encourage them to work.   How-ever, some are rated as neutral by their wives.

As mentioned earlier in the chapter, when the relatives' opinions of each of the 14 "stay at homes" are examined, we find that 12 have at least one important relative who prefers that she stay at home.[18]   In contrast, only four of the 43 employed women have any important relative who takes that position.[19]   These findings demonstrate that, for the most part, educated women in Bangalore do not go to work or "take up jobs" as it is termed,

TABLE 20—CURRENT STATUS OF RESPONDENTS BY ATTITUDES OF SELECTED FAMILY MEMBERS

Family Attitudes	Working or Seeking Work		Studying		At Home	
	No.	%	No.	%	No.	%
Father						
Encourages work	24	59	8	40	1	8
Is neutral	14	34	11	55	5	42
Prefers her home	3	7	1	5	6	50
Total	41	100	20	100	12	100
Mother						
Encourages work	24	51	13	57	2	14
Is neutral	17	36	8	35	4	29
Prefers her home	6	13	2	9	8	57
Total	47	100	23	101	14	100
Brother 1						
Encourages work	17	61	9	47	4	50
Is neutral	10	36	8	42	2	25
Prefers her home	1	4	2	11	2	25
Total	28	101	19	100	8	100
Husband						
Encourages work	9	90	1	100	0	00
Is neutral	1	10	0	0	4	44
Prefers her home	0	0	0	0	5	56
Total	10	100	1	100	9	100

(a) $N = 95$. Totals represent living family members who are considered as having influence by the respondent. Opinions which could not be classified according to the scale are omitted. Precentages vary slightly from Table 19, in which $N = 97$.

(b) One future husband of an engaged woman is included.

without the agreement of their parents or husbands, if married.

We noted that there are 14 women who say they would prefer not to work if there were no financial need. Relatives of this group of 14 are not as strongly against work as are those of the 14 who do not work. Less than half of the first group have at least one important relative who prefers that she stay at home. The desire to remain at home, then, need not be a reflection of family views. On the other hand, some parents may have reluctantly permitted their daughters to work due to economic circumstances, without considering it desirable. Or they might insist that the woman work if her earnings are needed.

Those women, who are studying for advanced degrees tend to report that their families' views are permissive more often than do others. Although such families have not yet had to face the immediate prospect of the daughter's employment, they are not likely to oppose it. This is borne out from Table 20 which shows that very low percentages of families having a daughter in advanced studies take the position that they would prefer her to remain at home.

It is interesting to note the degree of family consensus about whether or not a daughter should work. Since opinions on the matter appear to be changing, we may expect some disagreement among members of the same family. Agreement and disagreement within a family can be assessed by pairing each family member with the others.[20] Disagreement is rated mild if two members hold adjacent viewpoints on the five-point scale described on page 101. It is rated strong if their views are more than two intervals apart. Averaging the paired agreements and disagreements of all family members, the average rate of agreement is 59 per cent, of mild disagreement only 5 per cent, and of strong disagreement 26 per cent. Degree of agreement could not be judged in an average of 4 per cent of the pairings.

Only 38 families are found in which all members whose views are known are in agreement. Looking at the status of respondents in these families, 20 are working, 11 are studying, five are seeking work, and two are at home. Apparently family consensus is not required for a daughter to remain at home, but is necessary in order to support the departure from custom represented by employment. All but three of the families which are unanimous in their views either encourage or are permissive of the woman's working. The neutral or permissive position on the part of her family is evidently all that is needed to enable a young woman to work.

Only two cases occur in which the family prefers a daughter to remain at home but still allows her to work or to seek work. Economic necessity may be the reason for their behavior. It is also likely that once it has become necessary for a woman to work, the family will find reasons to support and justify her doing so.

Family size and composition undoubtedly affect the degree of agreement and disagreement found among its members. A more detailed analysis of family opinions would have to consider such questions as the relative authority of various members, the birth position of siblings, and the presence or absence of fathers or brothers. The possibilities for disagreement are, of course, greater if more family members are entering into discussion. On the average, a smaller number of family members' opinions were presented for comparison in those families where there was agreement on the issue of women's employment than was true of all families. However, if the views of the second and third brothers are excluded from all family comparisons, the total number of families which are in agreement does not change.

The paired comparisons of family members do not reveal dramatic alignments based solely on age or sex. The second eldest brother varies from the eldest in his alignment of views. The presence of a second eldest brother (as occurred in more than a third of the cases) may be important in families in which there is already dissensus. While brother one and brother three are more often in agreement with the father than with their sisters, brother two shows greater agreement with the sisters. On the subject under discussion, he shares the views of his father less often than those of any other family member, a pattern in which he resembles sisters rather than brothers. However, a proportionately higher percentage of brother two's differences with other family members are described as mild rather than strong in nature.

Almost half of the sisters disagree with either their fathers or mothers, or both. This evidence of independent thinking might not be readily observable, since their views are being reported by the respondents, their sisters. In fact, these views may or may not be stated openly to elders. At any rate, since sisters are low in authority, their support of a woman who wants to work probably does not weigh heavily. It might be noted that one-third of the mothers disagree, either mildly or strongly, with the fathers. However, this does not mean that any of the disagreement will be made known outside of the family circle.

In countries where single women are free to work before marriage, such as in the United States, there has been continuing opposition to the employment of mothers. It is only in recent decades that mothers of young children have entered the labor force in large numbers.

India's case is different in some respects. For centuries many proscriptions were built around the need to protect the chastity and honor of the unmarried female. Employment was viewed as a hazard which exposed her to too many temptations and hence could sully her value and prevent the attainment of her most important future role, that of wife.

Employment : hindrance or help to woman's marital chances

In Chapter 4 (Table 13) it was observed that fewer than 40 per cent of respondents consider employment an asset in finding a suitable mate. Another 38 per cent view employment as neither positive nor negative, and only about one-quarter of them feel it is harmful to marital chances. The hypothesis that norms against the employment of single females have weakened among this urban group is supported by our data.

It was also noted (Table 14, Chapter 4) that the most frequently mentioned explanation of the benefits of employment was that the bride could help her husband economically. Those who believe that boys' families prefer employed girls mention the high cost of living and the fact that families need several wage-earners.

In contrast, respondents who still consider employment a hindrance in marital desirability mention the negative character traits attributed to employed women. A Brahmin who is staying at home after receiving her B.A. states, "It is a hindrance. Our community feels it is a hindrance. Boys' parents think the girl is not domestic and doesn't know anything about the house." And a married woman agrees with this point of view saying, "It hinders. Indians are not so broad-minded to accept employed girls. They will have some bad opinion. They think the girls are careless and character-less." A related opinion is given by a Christian, who holds a law degree, as follows :

It depends—there are still certain families who like to think that the incoming daughter has not ventured beyond the four walls, except to a girl's institution and back. Teaching would be least objectionable.

Thus, a number of women feel that an employed female might still be expected to evidence such negative traits as questionable moral character, lack of domesticity, or too much independence. The surprising fact is that so few share these views.

Work participation of married respondents in 1967 and in 1977

The small group of 19 married women in the sample will be examined to see if marital status is a determining factor in whether or not an educated woman works. Somewhat fewer than one-third of the married women, compared to 49 per cent of the single ones, are working. The young wife who is seeking employment may be presumed to have the support of her husband, since she would be unlikely to go against his wishes. If we include the women who are seeking employment as well as those now employed, the picture changes. Ten of the married women (53 per cent) and 42 (55 per cent) of the single women may be considered available for the labor force.

In 1977 we find that over 40 per cent of the married women in the follow-up study are working. There is a close correspondence between the husband's reported attitude and whether or not his wife is actually working. Almost 60 per cent of the respondents indicate that their husbands prefer them to stay at home. In many cases, however, they cite additional reasons for not working : the posting of their husbands to areas in which job opportunities for educated women are not available, the lack of suitable persons for child care, and no economic need to work.

Views about the employment of mothers and childless married women

The fact that work is not proscribed for married women may seem less surprising if one recognizes that divorce is almost nonexistent in India, that duty toward one's husband is a prime value, and that the married woman, being sexually satisfied, is presumed to be less vulnerable. Thus she may safely be given more freedom than her single sisters. What of the young mother?

In 1967, we speculate on the question of whether or not the birth of a child puts an end to participation in the labor force, based upon the experience of the seven mothers in the sample. Of the seven, four are working, and one is trying hard to obtain work. An additional young mother has just been delivered of her first child and is not in a position to work. On the other hand, of the 12 married but childless women, half are neither working, seeking work, nor studying. Thus a higher proportion of mothers than of childless wives are working or seeking work. In 1977, only 2 of the 25 married (or separated) women do not as yet have children; both are working. However, of the working mothers, more than half have children under the age of 5.[21]

Financial reasons may well be involved in the employment of mothers. As we will see below, respondents in the original sample strongly support the participation of mothers in the labor force when economically necessary. In addition, the Indian wife who has borne a child acquires more prestige within her new family, and may be given greater freedom. Although in-law families are critically observant of the young bride in her apprenticeship days, they may loosen the reins once she has proven herself by having a child. As can be seen in Table 21, respondents, who undoubtedly recognize the pressures on new brides, strongly favor the right of the childless woman to work, and thereby to escape the possible opprobrium of anxious parents-in-law.

Asked to define the conditions under which they think that a married woman who has no children should work, only two individuals categorically state that married women should not work.

Table 21 shows that a different major reason serves to justify the employment of childless wives as compared to mothers. "To keep herself occupied" is mentioned most frequently for the childless wives and least frequently for mothers. Financial reasons are overwhelmingly stressed in explaining why a mother may work, and they are second in importance for childless wives. These answers suggest that views about women's employment are closely related to, rather than in conflict with, their family roles. The cultural implication of childlessness is that it is a condition to be pitied. Many answers reveal the belief that a childless woman is subject to brooding and unhappiness if she is not kept busy. A childless marriage does not constitute a fulfilled family role for the wife, and she is expected to need outside interests to compensate for the loss. In phrasing this question the Western practice, where wives frequently postpone motherhood in order to work for a short while, was an obvious influence. However, the phrase, "a married woman without children," has a different meaning in India. Here are some typical comments, the first by a 22-year-old non-Brahmin Hindu, who says, "If the family worries her too much about her not getting children, and she takes it to heart, it is better to work, to keep her mind engaged. If not, and she be quite rich, she may do some social services."

A Brahmin M.A. voices similar sentiments : "If she feels frustrated and sad and that she is wasting her time without doing any useful work, I feel she should work outside the home."

And a Moslem M.A. expresses the same point of view : "It is better for her to work outside the home. Thus, she would be engaged and it will lessen the idea of the loss."

The vast majority of the sample believes that mothers should work if

TABLE 21—RESPONDENTS' VIEWS OF CONDITIONS UNDER WHICH
MARRIED WOMEN OR MOTHER MAY WORK

Condition	Married, no children		Mother	
	No.	%	No.	%
Keep self occupied	61	44	2	2
If financial difficulties arise	39	28	77	66
If she likes	10	7	4	3
Make use of education; do something useful	10	7	3	3
If husband allows	10	7	—	—
If someone looks after household and children	—	—	15	13
If children are grown	—	—	9	8
Other	9	7	6	5
Total	139	100	116	100

there is economic need. As is true of most societies, a mother's role is supposed to include emotional support and personal care of her children — except if the individual is compelled to sacrifice these emotional components for more pressing economic needs. Widowhood, absence of male economic support, and destitution have always been a part of life in India; it is far from uncommon for women to support their children. Today, the cost of living and desire for decent standards by the middle class help to include women from this class in the ranks of the employed. Viewed in this light, work is a support for, rather than a threat to, the family.

Representatives of the three religious groups in our sample express their reasoning on the matter as follows.

A 23-year-old non-Brahmin Hindu doctor states simply, "A mother can work outside whenever their material resources are not enough to lead a better life."

A 21-year-old Christian justifies employment this way : "To meet the financial problems [she can work]. To give better comforts to her children."

And a Moslem M.A. says, "Only if she has no other source to bring up her children, or if the husband's income is less, to keep up the standard of living."

Other conditions mentioned receive many fewer responses.   One-fifth of the answers include the provision that the mother's working should not adversely affect her children.   A tiny 4 per cent of those interviewed categorically state that a mother should not work.   However, an equally small percentage of responses permissive of employment would allow a mother to work "if she likes" or "to keep self occupied," reasons which suggest personal interests.   Such reasons might be added after a set of more compelling ones, as in this answer given by a working mother of two :

First, if separated or widowed.   Second, financial.   If she's interested, it's all right too, just for interest—even if she's rich.   My mother takes care of my children, so it's not as if a servant were there.

A Brahmin Ph.D. candidate was one of the few who mentions use of the mother's talents for society at large rather than just for the family's benefit :

First consideration is financial.   Second is if the mother is a woman of talents and intellect, her usefulness should not be confined only to her home.   It could be utilized to improve our nation in any manner.

It should be noted that this viewpoint is very rare and is not fully accepted even in highly industrialized societies such as the United States. In 1967, attitudinal data about work seems unrelated to the caste or religious background of sample members.   Rosen's (1966) assertion that class divisions begin to assume more importance than caste in the city is supported by these findings, for the group under study.[22]   Still, our new information suggests that Brahmin wives may be less likely to work than their counterparts from other religious and caste groups.   Further study is needed to test this hypothesis.

A developing issue : the strain of combining work and home roles

In the literature on Indian working women, increasing attention has been focused on two issues : the waste of educated womanpower when jobs are either unavailable or women do not seek them; and the problem of strain brought about as women carry on their traditional home duties, adding to them the obligations of outside work.   India's working wives are experiencing a world-wide pattern, what Professor Nona Glazer calls, "the normalization of the double day."[23]   The persistence of traditional norms in regard to women's domestic roles is particularly strong in India with husbands frequently expecting many personal services and refusing to share in household tasks (Government of India, 1974 : 88).

In her extensive studies of the marital adjustment of educated working wives, Kapur found that a significant factor in creating marital disharmony was the clash between a husband's patriarchal attitude and his wife's equalitarian one.   Many men appear to have ambivalent feelings about their educated wives, and make incongruous demands (Kapur, 1974, Chap. 2).   To illustrate : one member of our 1977 sample comments bitterly about a husband who wants the added income of a working wife but resents her association with other males at work, demands that she perform domestic duties excellently, and criticizes her level of child care. Others, too, write more generally about the difficulty in combining work and home roles.   However, disagreement within marriage is unlikely to lead to separation or divorce except in extreme cases.   One such case appears to have occurred in the follow-up sample, where the partners are separated.   When women have no independent means of support they are unable to leave an unhappy or difficult marriage.   A number of them are deserted, however, and of course many Indian women eventually face widowhood.   For women who are alone, employment may be essential.

Separation and divorce are stigmatized by many Hindu communities, but recent research suggests that they occur with greater frequency than is publicly acknowledged.   During her studies of educated employed women, Rama Mehta met several who were divorced.   Through them she was able to locate 50 separated or divorced women, whom she interviewed in depth.   She found that those who had careers were best adjusted to their marital situation, and all wanted to work (Mehta, 1975).

In the next chapter, we address the issue of how educated womanpower is used.   Educated women have a potential for employment, but finding jobs deemed suitable is not always easy.   The issue is seen as a compelling one by respondents in 1967, and again in 1977.   Half of the latter group make specific reference to unemployment or the difficulty in finding jobs. Chapter 6 takes a closer look at the definition of work that is "suitable" and provides factual data about the jobs held by these women.

CHAPTER 6

FINDING A SUITABLE JOB

Patterns of female employment

STUDIES document the variability in patterns of female employment, even among countries which are at the same stage of industrialization.[1] Surveying women's role in economic development cross-culturally, Boserup (1970 : 69-73) finds differing patterns in societies which practise female seclusion and those which do not. The participation of women in the labor force is, of course, much lower in the former than in the latter societies. Particular occupations or professions which are favored as women's fields in some countries and regions are looked down upon in others.

In times of national emergency, dramatic breakdowns in the sexual division of labor may take place. Under other circumstances, such as a changing economy, norms defining jobs for women are modified much more slowly. To look at one occupation as an example, nursing has been a highly preferred field for women in many countries but has been stigmatized in India and other parts of Asia. The following interpretation has been given :

... in many parts of Asia, parents object to their daughters becoming nurses. In India, the objection is partly because nurses violate caste rules by handling bedpans, and partly because nurses must go out for night work or live outside the family premises, which is considered indecent in many Indian families. Thus, most recruits for Indian nursing schools are low-caste girls or Anglo-Indian girls . . . (Boserup, 1970 : 130).

There is evidence, nonetheless, that the number of nurses in India has increased over the past two decades. The expansion of health services has made more jobs available, and better training opportunities in nursing schools and colleges have been created. This combination of factors gives nursing a more favorable image, and serves to increase the number of women entering it (Government of India, 1974 : 207).

The field of social work has had status as an avocation, providing an outlet for the talents of a small group of educated, elite, sometimes powerful, women. Such leaders perform the work of executives without pay, and may be active in the ranks of social reformers.   Many women political leaders have come from this group. But while *paid* social work is a favored female occupation in many countries, it has not been so regarded in India. At the time of the original study the school of social work in Bangalore had not yet been granted formal governmental accreditation; its graduates received a technical diploma rather than a degree.[2] This lack of status reflected the little recognition accorded to paid social work in Bangalore.[3] We predicted that this situation might change because of a number of factors: the presence of highly regarded schools of social work as models in a few major Indian cities, the high educational and professional qualifications of the director of the Bangalore school, and the need for trained social workers in promoting the national goal of family planning. Although we do not have specific data on Bangalore, national statistics indicate an increase in the number of paid female social workers.[4]

Library science was seen as another possible source of employment for educated women. It, too, had not received recognition in Bangalore at the time of the initial research. One respondent who was studying this subject expected to receive a technical diploma rather than the more valuable advanced degree. Library science is not mentioned as a significant avenue for female employment in recent works. An increase in library resources would, of course, be needed to create more training and job opportunities.

Medicine is referred to as an early aspiration by some members of the sample. This field has been "an accepted and respected profession for women for a considerable period" (Government of India, 1974 : 207). The opening of medical education to women was an early goal of Indian reform, deemed essential if women's health were to be improved.[5] Unsurprisingly, women doctors have, until recent times, tended to concentrate in the fields of obstetrics and gynecology. Although they now enter some other specialties, their clients continue to be mainly women and children.

Teaching is a preferred occupation for women in most countries of the world. In India, as elsewhere, the hours of teaching and system of vacations free women to devote comparatively more time to children and household than do other jobs. This, as well as its obvious respectability, helps to account for teaching's popularity. Boserup notes that, despite the existence of wide differences in attitudes toward women's roles, professions appear to be open to educated women as well as educated men in African, Arab, Asian and American countries. Considering the matter further, she finds that in most countries two-thirds or more of all women in the pro-

While there is a fairly wide range of salaries among both of female seclu-loyees and teachers, their average salaries differ. The median income teachers, if we include college lecturers with others, is between 150 and 199 rupees per month, while the median income of those in clerical positions falls in the range of 200 to 249 rupees. However, no college teacher earns less than 200 rupees.[8] The best paid clerical jobs are held by two women with bachelor of law degrees. Only two-fifths of the clerical workers earn as little as 199 rupees. The two physicians are obviously at the top of the income scale. At the bottom, eight teachers earn under 150 rupees and are the only workers earning so little.

Of the teachers of all types, 56 per cent hold a degree past the first bachelor's degree, whereas only one-third of the 15 clerical workers hold such degrees. Thus, while the average education of teachers is higher, their average salary is lower. However, matching up education with income, there is a significant correlation. Two-thirds of those holding only a B.A. or B.Sc. earn below 200 rupees per month, while three-quarters of those holding higher degrees earn above 200 rupees per month. The general belief that advanced education increases one's earning power is borne out by the facts, and is evidently true for both sexes.

The expression of general attitudes about work and the problems of educated working women tended to be offered more freely than answers about the respondent's own job. An individual respondent would more willingly point out that salaries are not commensurate with women's education than discuss the fact that her own salary was low.[9] This reticence to talk negatively about one's own job can be explained in several ways. First, the overwhelmingly positive orientation to work rather than the alternative of sitting at home may encourage women to suppress minor dissatisfactions. Second, women have been taught that it is up to them to adjust to what is required and demanded, rather than complain. Third, there is the matter of pride and the belief that one should not engage in activities below one's status or educational qualifications. A job deemed unsuitable may be rejected even in cases of prolonged unemployment. If it is accepted, excuses may be made to save face. Finally, the formal interview situation probably inhibited some individuals from openly criticizing their jobs. However, in informal conversations held with young women other than respondents, criticism also centered about conditions of employment and rates of pay rather than intrinsic aspects of their work.

Employment problems of educated women

The interviewees were asked to describe the employment problems of educated women, if they believed such to exist. Twenty per cent maintain that it is not difficult for graduates to get work and envision no other problems. A few believe that there are some difficulties but cannot elaborate. Seventy-one describe one or more types of problems encountered by educated women, totalling 119 responses. These fall into several major categories : (1) the unavailability of appropriate jobs—26 per cent of responses; (2) the need for special types of qualifications, such as typing—25 per cent; (3) the use of criteria other than merit in determining appointments—20 per cent; (4) the general problem of unemployment—12 per cent; and (5) family and societal pressures on women who work—8 per cent. The remaining responses are vague or miscellaneous.

Paucity of Jobs "Suitable" for Women

The highest percentage of answers concentrate in the area of the appropriateness of available jobs. Under this category are included statements about the inconvenience of hours or work places for women; the unsuitability of some work environments; the fact that salaries do not measure up to educational attainments; and the failure of available jobs to utilize one's education. Within this category, then, we find references to the problems of the educated in general and others which apply more specifically to women.

There is a strong implication in answers that it is demeaning to accept work which is beneath one's qualifications even if it be white collar work. In Indian society, as suggested, educated persons are familiar with the rank of job for which they qualify, especially since specific educational requirements are attached to government jobs. The large percentage of positions in the public sector, with clear-cut formal criteria of selection, enable the individual to assess the gap between jobs for which he is eligible and those which are available. One of the Indian interviewers, summarizing the views of a young Christian woman who holds a bachelor of law degree, writes :

Her main problem was expressed with regard to her education and her job. She said that she hates to call herself a clerk after doing the Bachelor of Law. She expressed the view that after doing postgraduate study one would like to occupy a respectable position and not be called a clerk, which is looked down upon in society. With respect to what she liked least about her job, she said that though she took so much pains in drafting letters, she couldn't subscribe her signature on them. Thus she felt her importance is not felt.[10]

In the teaching field, too, jobs are ranked in terms of prestige. Since possession of a master's degree qualifies one to be a college lecturer, some of those holding such degrees express the sentiment that teaching in a high school is beneath them. A Moslem M. A., holding out for college teaching or research as the only appropriate work, explains her situation in this way :[11]

> I want to do teaching or research. I want only college teaching. Yes, I have tried at the government colleges. I want to do a Ph.D., but that, too, is difficult. Even though my family is educated, even to my grandfather, still our religion influences things. The girls can't go out freely. Some of the jobs require working with many kinds of people, like social work or family planning. My family would allow only teaching or research. That is what I prefer.

However, some women are beginning to question the attitudes expressed above. One who is studying for a bachelor's degree in education maintains that such feelings are due to the lack of dignity accorded to work. She states :

> Another problem is the fact that many educated girls scorn jobs because they feel they are too lowly in nature and acceptance of them will result in a loss of status. Girls should be taught the dignity of labor, which should be emphasized in colleges. This will prevent the waste of so much talent and education.

This concern with an appropriately prestigious job for his daughter is expressed by a father as he suggests that women are discriminated against :

> There is still difficulty in getting suitable jobs. She is teaching in a primary school near here, but it is not very good. It is only till she gets a better job. She put her name in the Employment Exchange over a year ago. Only one offer came in and it was not satisfactory. The Exchanges don't work so well. Many government offices are not hiring women. It is changing but it is still difficult.

Clerical work is rejected frequently because of the view that offices lack the "proper atmosphere" for women. A Brahmin teacher who resides with her brother and sister-in-law states, "My brothers don't like me to work in an office. I, too, like teaching . . . Many girls are working in factories where the atmosphere is not nice." And a respondent who works as a clerk puts it this way : "If a girl gets a job, she must consider first whether it is a proper place. If there are rowdies there, she won't go. A boy can work anywhere, but in India a girl can't."

Another woman studying for her bachelor of education degree explained that she had been offered a job through the government Employment Exchange but "since it was clerical" she did not accept it.

The number of clerical workers is too small for detailed analysis, but it might be noted that none of the employed Moslem women are working in offices. Brahmins are also less well-represented than other castes in these posts.

Issue of Job Location

Underlying assumptions about the special difficulties of members of their sex, as well as references to general employment problems are reflected in the interviews quoted above. Two women who hold master's degrees describe the problems of women very specifically, both stressing the issue of job location. The first, a Brahmin studying for her Ph.D. states :

I feel there is not much of a problem to get a job in Bangalore. But the suitability of environment or working conditions and the distances weigh much in a girl taking up employment. There are many jobs but the problem is one of transport and environment. There are many jobs in banks, but our Indian girls are rather shy, and they may not feel right if there are no other girls and many men. With some jobs, the hours are not so convenient. Work may end at 5:30, but with the buses she may not get home until eight. Most girls like to work in offices. The burden is not too much, and it is shared. The government jobs are more secure. But if they are lecturers in government colleges, there is the problem of being transferred.

And the other M.Sc. points out,

If they get a job, there is the question of whether it is in Bangalore or out of Bangalore. Which type of job she gets—it may be in her line or out of her line. She may prefer to stay in Bangalore. Even if the job is out of her line she may prefer to work in Bangalore. She may take into consideration other facts—facilities, hostel or house in a nice place, the type of living there.   She has to consider all these things.

Once again, the problem of finding respectable living quarters away from home is articulated.   This problem is recognized in the Education Commission's proposal that more attention be given to developing hostels for teachers.   Parents who agree to allow their daughter to take an out-of-town post may send along an elderly female relative as chaperone.

Proximity to home is frequently a significant factor in the family's decisions about a daughter's educational activities or place of work.   The hypothesis might be tested that permitted distance between home and work is an index of the conservatism of the family.   The relative prestige of the position may prove to be a counter-balancing factor, however.

The inconvenience and delay of public transportation in Bangalore is a proper excuse for any late arrival for appointments.   In addition to the discomfort of long queues, overcrowded and off-schedule buses, there is the matter of returning home late in the evening.   And of course the hours kept by a single woman will be scrutinized by neighbors.   For those most orthodox, the girl's absence at work signifies that she is away from parental supervision and perhaps in the company of men.   If, in addition, she returns home beyond the hour considered proper, her reputation may suffer.

The unmarried daughter is sometimes expected to eat her meals at home, a difficult requirement if her job is any distance away.   Most middle class individuals observe the custom of going home for lunch or of having hot meals brought to their place of work by a family servant or special functionary.[12]

The importance of eating meals prepared in one's own kitchen is great. There are caste prescriptions and taboos about who may handle food, and much distaste for unfamiliar cooking.   Family, religious, and caste styles of food preparation vary, and some Hindus do not like to eat food in cafeterias and restaurants.   At the same time, hot meals are very much preferred.   Most restaurants, except for a few expensive ones, are considered out of bounds to respectable women.   They may be suspected of arranging a rendezvous with a man there.   The expense of eating lunch out in a decent place is exorbitant.[13]   A working woman's dilemma of where and how to have lunch is solved in several ways. Some parents restrict daughters to jobs near home, so that lunch can be taken in the usual fashion. Some Hindus eat a very early lunch before starting out for work, which frequently begins at 10 a.m.   Offices may set working hours in such a manner as to include a long lunch period so that workers are able to travel home for their meal. Shops are frequently closed for two or three hours in mid-day.

The status of a job may determine the degree of time flexibility tolerated. Unmarried physicians are allowed to maintain unusual hours, since the prestige of the position is unquestioned.[14] Despite the greater permissiveness in this job category, place and conditions of work strongly influence the jobs that a respectable woman may take.

Need for Special Qualifications

Turning now to some of the other categories of problems mentioned, a quarter of the responses deal with special qualifications that are needed. Certain degrees are considered better than others in the employment market; the B. Sc., for example, is more valuable than B.A. A bachelor of education degree (making one a "double graduate") entitles its possessor to better teaching posts in secondary schools. A master's degree qualifies one for the position of college lecturer or a higher clerical post. In some cases a degree is not sufficient in itself, and merit, in the form of graduating in the upper part of one's class is needed. A number of individuals spoke of a third class master's degree as being less valuable than a bachelor's degree.[15] However, "merit" was mentioned specifically as a special qualification only eight times. The role of influence was noted more frequently.

Among other special qualifications, almost a third of the responses indicate the value of technical skills such as typing or shorthand. Respondents spoke of taking up typing as a "side study" which would prove useful in obtaining employment.[16]

Role of Influence : Caste, Sex and other Discriminations

A fifth of the responses dealing with problems in work suggest that criteria other than merit are used in hiring applicants. The role of influence is mentioned far more often than any other criterion, such as sex, caste or religion. The term "influence" is used broadly and often includes within it the notion that considerations of caste or religion are significant. It sometimes serves as a euphemism for these terms, but may mean that family connections carry much weight. One respondent spoke proudly of obtaining a teaching post on her own even though her mother could readily have obtained one for her.

A Christian woman, working as an upper division clerk in a government factory was more explicitly critical of caste than most :

India is not much progressed. Employment opportunities are few. Moreover, in the government offices itself they have this caste feeling and are very prejudiced. First thing they enquire about is caste. We can't talk about private concerns but the government itself does. It means there is no way for others to come up. Some people, though they don't possess any intelligence, will occupy high positions. Whereas brilliant students do not get, because of caste. I agree if they consider merit as the main criteria, but not caste.

And a wealthy Moslem woman, married to a physician, complains of religious prejudice :

As far as my case is concerned, I think that being a minority—i.e., a Muslim—is a great setback in obtaining a job. Proof is that I, standing first in the University, could not get a job after applying in six colleges. That is why I'm very keen on going abroad and doing my Ph.D., and working abroad.[17]

Most respondents were less direct in mentioning caste influence, a topic which came up more frequently in informal contacts. However, some respondents did complain that the official preference given to members of Scheduled Castes, through compensatory legislation, made things more difficult for members of other castes. As mentioned previously, only two members of the sample turn out to be from this "privileged" group. Those interviewed did not mention specifically another caste group which is highly influential in the city, and which is reputedly able to obtain preference for its own members in various appointments. This group, too, was not highly represented in the sample.

Discrimination on the basis of sex is barely mentioned. The following hypotheses may be offered : first, educated women presently compete with men in very few fields since they confine themselves to lower clerical posts and teaching. They are also considered essential in dealing with members of their own sex, so that, for example, female doctors have a natural clientele and are not considered unusual. The whole field of family planning is also one that requires not only trained workers but women, especially to serve members of their own sex. In order to recruit them, government becomes increasingly concerned with providing proper living quarters and incentives. Pressure is also exerted by the government Employment Exchanges, as they continue to offer family planning jobs to any qualified woman who places her name in the Exchange. However, as women seek positions in fields more traditionally male oriented, they may encounter more opposition.[18]

Secondly, the prevalence of other societal divisions seems to supercede that of sex, as in the case of the Moslem respondent quoted earlier. She interprets discrimination against her to be based on religion rather than sex or marital status. Women are now able to obtain a number of government jobs for which formal education requirements are strongly emphasized. The same patterns of sexual discrimination in employment that one finds in a country such as the United States may not develop in India. The middle class women who take jobs based on their educational qualifications will be fitted into a stratified employment system based on those qualifications, aided or hindered by caste and family connections. Thus, sex may play a minor role in obtaining positions.

At present women are criticized for their shyness and unwillingness to enter untraditional fields, but should they try to enter male domains, such as engineering, there might be opposition. In contrast, a small number of elite women have succeeded in playing important roles in Indian history. Such women may enter politics, as they enter social work, as a duty to serve others. The advantages of coming from leading political families, and having excellent education, may enable some women to operate as equals in the political sphere. Within the home a woman has a prescribed relationship to her father and husband—males of the same family position. Outside the home, the woman's class and caste position have much to do with how she treats members of other classes and castes, regardless of sex.

The role of sex in determining appropriate fields of study may also work to the educated woman's advantage in that the best male students are drawn off to medicine and engineering. This means that, for example, in a field such as sociology, women students may predominate and may perform better than their male co-students. They are more likely to do well on examinations and present good records in seeking employment if they are competing with men who were not able to obtain seats in more desirable fields. Thirdly, the Central Government has been trying to equalize the position of women and has opened up new educational and employment opportunities. Government enterprises, such as arts and crafts emporia, employ many of them, some in managerial positions. A series of legal reforms has attempted to equalize the legal rights of women. Remuneration for particular government posts is standardized, so that women will receive the same rate of pay as men.

A little more than a tenth of the responses about problems in work prefer to the general problem of unemployment.   Concern about the large number of the "educated unemployed" young people in India has been voiced in many quarters.[19] As colleges open their doors to more students, and as these graduate, the problem becomes more severe.   Respondents who express concern over unemployment usually feel that opportunities should be improved for both men and women.   One young woman who is studying for her master's degree in economics has a different opinion, stating,

It is hard for boys to get employment. That's one of our big problems in India.   So I don't think girls should work unless there is financial difficulty.   For example, a girl took up a post here and left after one year.   That took up a place a boy could have had.   For us it is not so important, as we won't be the main financial support, but for a boy, he will work all his life, so it is important for him. That's what I think. I don't know how others feel [said somewhat defensively]. It is easier for girls to get jobs.

Hers was definitely a minority viewpoint.

Ten persons specify that there are still family and societal pressures against women working, such as the ones already discussed. At the same time, there are ways in which these pressures are being counterbalanced. The family which needs the daughter's salary to maintain its standard of living allows her to take a "suitable" job, or even comes to view a respectably employed daughter-in-law as an asset. As work becomes more usual, it also becomes more acceptable. Then, when the more desirable types of jobs are unavailable, women may be permitted to work in somewhat less satisfactory surroundings, as in the case of this government factory clerk. She comments, "Father didn't want me to join the factory but there is no other job. I applied in X Bank, but didn't get, because a lot of recommendation is needed there."

As more middle class women enter the ranks of the educated and subsequently the employed, further modifications of norms will gradually take place. A daughter who has taught in a neighborhood school may be allowed to accept a better position some distance away from home. Parents whose daughters have worked as teachers may permit one of them to take a slightly less suitable job.

Such changes in parental attitudes are described by a number of women. As daughters acquire the qualifications for prestigious positions, and the boldness to argue for them, the titles and salary begin to outweigh past objections. In 1967 we anticipated further gradual change — an increase in the kinds of work in which middle class women may engage and less restriction as to place of work.

Work satisfaction and dissatisfaction

Working respondents were given a range of choices with which to describe their jobs in terms of convenience or inconvenience (with regard to work, time and place) and how interesting and tiring they are. They were also asked the extent to which they felt that their education had prepared them for the job, what they specifically liked or disliked, and what other job they might prefer. Table 23 compares the responses of different types of workers, and of those earning higher and lower salaries, to some of these questions.

Even though the location of work place and hours of work are important considerations in choice of jobs, they are not always found to be satisfactory. Forty-five per cent of the respondents feel that either place or hours of work are inconvenient. There is a significant difference between the convenience ratings of teachers and clerks, a finding that is not surprising.[20] The possibility of obtaining work in a school that is near one's home is fairly good, since schools are located in many different neighborhoods. Government office buildings and factories are less likely to be near the woman's residence. A much higher proportion of teachers than clerks report that their work is very interesting, the difference being statistically significant.[21] Teachers find their work more tiring than do clerks; more than half of the latter consider their jobs "not at all tiring." This suggests that they may sometimes find themselves with too little to do. A question on boredom would undoubtedly have elicited more information on job satisfaction.

Over 80 per cent of the respondents feel that their education was very much needed, or somewhat needed, for their job, but the proportion is lower for clerks than for teachers. Even though clerks earn more, on the average, than teachers, they evidence less job satisfaction. There is a significant relationship between jobs described as very interesting and those for

TABLE 23—TYPE OF JOB AND SALARY EARNED BY RESPONDENT'S DESCRIPTION OF OWN JOB

Description of own job	Total		Physician		Teacher		Clerk		Salary under Rs. 200		Salary over Rs. 200	
	No.	%	No.	%	No.	%	No.	%	No.	%	No.	%
Total	42	100	2	100	25	100	15	100	19	100	23	100
Convenience of time and place of work												
1. Very convenient	22	52	0	0	18	72	4	27	10	53	13	57
2. Somewhat or very inconvenient	19	45	2	100	6	24	11	73	8	42	10	43
3. Not given	1	2	0	0	1	4	0	0	1	5	0	0
Whether work is tiring												
1. Very or somewhat	28	67	2	100	19	76	7	47	11	58	15	65
2. Not at all	14	33	0	0	6	24	8	53	8	42	8	35
Whether work is interesting												
1. Very	25	60	2	100	19	76	4	27	10	53	16	70
2. Somewhat or not at all	17	40	0	0	6	24	11	73	9	47	7	30
Whether her education was needed for job												
1. Very much or somewhat	34	81	2	100	23	92	9	60	15	79	19	83
2. Hardly or not at all	8	19	0	0	2	8	6	40	4	21	4	17

which one's education is considered relevant.[22] Six of the eight women who maintain that their education was hardly needed, or not needed at all, find their jobs uninteresting.

When we divide the working sample into those who earn above and below 200 rupees per month, we find fewer distinctive contrasts. Although a higher proportion of those earning higher salaries appear to find their work interesting, the relationship is not statistically significant.

The question of whether or not a woman's education is needed for her job was asked in a general way, and is subject to varying interpretations. A college degree may be required for a particular job, and in the formal sense then, the education is needed. Whether or not one actually uses what she has learned is also involved in this question. Respondents incorporated both interpretations into their answers. Future studies might profitably treat this subject in greater depth than was possible here. On-site observation of various work situations would prove useful.

Most respondents answer in very general terms when asked what they like or dislike most about work. The largest number (about one-third) say that they like teaching or teaching a particular subject, while almost 30 per cent mentioned contact with students or clients. Interaction with those they serve evidently provides more satisfaction than interaction with colleagues. Only a few women mention specific parts of their jobs—such as doing library work or writing reports — that are found enjoyable. Some would say no more than that they like everything about their work, and probing did not elicit more information.

In describing what they like least about their work, respondents stress factors other than contact with students or clients — even though "student indiscipline" is occasionally mentioned. Doing paper work of various sorts is the most disliked activity, and is frequently described as routine or uninteresting. Teachers are required to do much correcting of students' written work. Clerks in government offices may perform routine computations or mathematical work. Inconvenience of working place or times is mentioned again as a disliked aspect of work. A number of individuals insist that there is nothing that they dislike about their work. As has been suggested earlier, respondents are evidently reluctant to criticize their jobs. It may be, too, that "liking one's job" is not an important value and that other criteria such as the job's importance or the security provided by it are weighed much more heavily.

Lack of vocational involvement

Few individuals evidence a thoughtful approach to, or examination of, the work they are doing, nor do they provide much detail about their actual duties.   As noted in Chapter 4, their desire to work is not usually based upon interest in the intrinsic nature of a particular job.

Shils' observations about the approach of Indian intellectuals to their work are relevant here.   He asserts that Indians in intellectual professions are characterized by "vocational apathy" (Shils, 1961 : 25-26). Shils partially accounts for this by the explanation that professions are imposed on individuals rather than chosen freely, but also relates this stance to the minimization of worldly preoccupations in Indian culture. His generalizations are probably even truer for women, since work is more often thought of as a way of filling time or supplementing family income than as a focus of personal involvement.   This vocational apathy may lessen as women become more interested in their work or see it as a way of contributing to the nation. That critical interest in one's own field and in teaching methods can gradually grow is illustrated in this tale of her own development told by a young Brahmin college instructor :

The subjects are not taught in an interesting way.   I only became interested in zoology after taking my M.Sc.   My father wanted me to get married right after my B.Sc., but I didn't want, so I took up the M.Sc.   But I was not interested in the subject.   I only went to college to have good times, and many of us did.   I had no thought of continuing so I thought, "If I get third class, it's good enough."   I thought that I would never use my education.   I was lucky enough to get a second class, so I got a place and could go on . . . .
We have to teach in a way that is not interesting to the students and not interesting to us.   We should be able to teach generally first and comparatively. Instead we go into each part in a given order. There is a lot to cover, and that means in the third year everything is piled up . . . . The older people don't want to change the curriculum, but some of them are beginning to see the need for change.

A great devotion to task is perhaps more natural when it is tied in with a sense of religious mission.   A young Christian woman of the Pentecostal church, who has not been included in the working sample because her efforts are voluntary, might be quoted here :

I have chosen throughout my life to do social service and religious work, helping the poor and needy, advising the ignorant for a better and peaceful life, showing them the right way to hate evil habits and turn their minds towards God and to their daily duties.

Since this woman has rejected marriage as a goal, she finds no conflict between her religious efforts and other roles. Her remarks that she would marry if fate turned up a man with similar dedication sounded strangely similar to those made by women who said they would be willing to marry if it did not interrupt their education!

Career preferences

Working respondents were asked what jobs they might prefer to their present ones. While more than a third claim to be content with their own jobs, the most frequent alternative, named by about one-fifth, is work in a bank. Jobs in banks are considered "fashionable"—glamorous, remunerative and the newest kind of work permitted to their daughters by some middle-class families. "Research," which usually refers to work towards a Ph.D., is the next most frequent choise. Candidates for Ph.D.'s are paid a stipend, enabling the individual to earn as well as attain her doctorate. The early interest in medicine expressed by seven women at some point in their interviews, was not mentioned as an alternate career choice. Women answered this question in terms of other positions for which they felt qualified rather than in terms of their previous aspirations. Three of the respondents' mothers, as compared to two respondents, are or have been physicians; these figures suggest that medicine has a history of acceptability as a field for women.

At the time of the original study, attitudes about specific jobs can be summarized in this way : Clerical jobs are still not considered totally satisfactory; those in banks are deemed most prestigious and exciting. Teaching continues to be the most acceptable and respectable work for women, and college lecturers enjoy considerable prestige. Only a lucky few women end up in medicine, despite the fact that it is an early aspiration for many more of them. Research for a Ph.D. has a double advantage in that it satisfies the desire to continue one's education and at the same time brings in a stipend. Most respondents seemed resigned to work in the few fields open to them.

Jobs held by respondents in 1977

In 1977, fourteen of the 30 follow-up respondents are employed, and
one is a member of a religious order. More than 60 per cent of them are
teaching, one-third of these at colleges. Twenty-one per cent hold clerical
or white collar jobs. However, two positions represent relatively new and
desirable fields for women—that of bank officer and research scientist.
The research scientist is the most highly educated respondent, and as
mentioned in Chapter 4, is engaged to be married to a man of her own
choice from a different caste. The bank officer is another modern woman
who, in 1967, had selected her future marital partner and withstood
parental opposition to the match.

The working respondents were questioned about their current salaries.
The range is broad : from a low of between Rs. 250 to 299 per month
earned by a clerical worker to salaries of over Rs. 1,000 per month reported by four women.[23] The latter salaries are earned by the bank officer,
research scientist and two college teachers. All but two of the working
respondents earn at least Rs. 600 monthly; the median salary is between
Rs. 700 and 749.

The majority of those now staying at home have worked previously—
in the same types of jobs as most of the employed respondents, including
one who was a college lecturer. Another who resides in the United States
held a technical job in the health field there, prior to the birth of her
child. These women seem to follow a pattern observable in other countries—that of working prior to or in the early years of marriage. In some
cases, their husbands' assignments to other regions made it necessary for
women to give up jobs. In others, the problem of adequate child care
was an issue. However, the high educational and occupational attainment of their husbands also means that economic necessity is not a compelling factor in many cases.

A little more than half of these respondents indicate that they have been
able to achieve what they wanted to in the area of employment—and
among them are two women who now happily stay at home with their
children. Both suggest, though, that this is no longer the norm and that
many married women are working. When asked about the problems of
educated women more generally, the respondents name the following
difficulties : obtaining suitable work, obtaining salaries commensurate
with one's education, combining home and work roles, adjusting to joint

family living and less-educated family members, unemployment, and in a
few cases adjusting to demanding and inconsiderate husbands.

These problems are not very different from the ones envisioned by the
larger group of respondents in 1967. However, ten years of life experience have made some women cognizant of the stress involved in trying to
combine traditional family roles with employment. There is also the
beginning of a notion that the husband of a working wife must learn "to
adjust."

CHAPTER 7

CONCLUSION

Review of women's position in Indian history

THE position of women has varied throughout India's vast history.[1] Invasion, conquest and colonialism, interpretations and re-interpretations of sacred writings, the joint family system and the economics of marriage have all played a part in bringing Indian women to a state of formal and legal subservience condemned by Mahatma Gandhi, Raja Ram Mohan Roy, Annie Besant and other great reformers of this century.

Child marriage had become obligatory by the beginning of the Christian era, in order to prevent the vulnerable sex from falling into evil ways. By the nineteenth century, the low level of literacy found in India especially characterized its women. Not only was widow remarriage forbidden, but in some regions the practice of *sati* was viewed as the most noble demonstration of wifely loyalty. Women were considered to be dependent on men for life : first their fathers, then husbands, then sons. Those who accepted this definition of themselves most fully were idealized and respected for their uncomplaining devotion as wives and mothers. Some were able to develop significant influence within their formally inferior roles, undoubtedly as a product of their artful sensitivity to the needs and whims of men. Thus, informal power was sometimes achieved, especially by the older women who ruled over domestic life. The lot of the new bride was frequently especially hard.

Then came the Independence Movement when, for the sake of the nation, and in line with their characteristic selflessness, Indian women forsook their homes to join in public demonstrations and to share the risk of arrest and imprisonment. Since Independence, elevating the position of women has become a major national goal. Well-known leaders provided ideological support to counter traditional prejudices. The Central Government instituted legislative reforms to increase educational opportunities and provide economic rights for women.

However, national goals do not constitute current reality. A number of dialectically interacting elements, including economic and cultural ones, are involved in the changes necessary to attain planned or desired goals. For example, it has been stressed that economic development tends to displace women of the lower socio-economic classes from their traditional work even as it provides employment opportunities for urban educated ones.

It is this latter category of women which we have studied in depth in the first and revised, updated work. Members of a stratified sample of all 1965 women graduates and post-graduates of Bangalore University were interviewed in 1966-67 (the "1967 sample"). Most are the first female generation in their families to attend college. They are termed "transitional" because their lives are much influenced by traditional norms and yet they are forerunners in carving out new roles for women. They have more contact with the world beyond the home than their less-educated middle class sisters. In a sample which includes Hindus from various communities, Moslems and Christians, we find that many of their concerns and life conditions are alike.[2] Other studies of highly educated women cited throughout this book depict similar problems and issues. One which has been referred to frequently is *Towards Equality*, the important report of the Committee on the Status of Women in India. This document builds upon other studies as well as original surveys, and provides a comprehensive analysis as well as proposals for the future.

Our own study examines the intermeshing of the educational and marriage systems as they affect the lives of our respondents. In doing so, it becomes clear that tradition is composed of many and sometimes conflicting elements, that some norms are congruent with changing conditions while others are not. For example, opportunities for female education help to raise the age at marriage—yet, even with an increase in female education, dowry practices persist.

Education of women—a bridge to employment

In our earlier (1972) book, we noted that many of those in our sample were working or would work, another new role for middle class women. To follow up on this and other predictions, we surveyed the same sample by questionnaire ten years after the first study. Encountering expected difficulty in locating correct addresses, we obtained responses from 31 per cent of the original group.[3] We found that 80 per cent of those in the follow-up have worked or are currently working. In some cases, employment was a temporary measure, preceding marriage or motherhood. Others are now working mothers.

It has been shown that the system of arranged marriage and traditional notions about women affect their entrance into college, but that college itself creates unintended consequences. Young women desire to extend this period of relative freedom from responsibility through further education or "taking up" a job. Those interviewed valued college attendence greatly, hoped to do advanced study, and recommended education to other women. Among urban families already convinced of the importance of education for their sons, "putting" daughters in college was becoming convenient and necessary. Faced with an older marriage age, the increased availability of college education, the delays involved in arranging marriage and accumulating dowry, and the quest of highly educated men for graduate brides, parents were finding college a worthwhile way of keeping their daughters busy. Traditional notions about women's sexuality led to the belief that they must be kept fully occupied. Parents could be less anxious about finding a bridegroom if their daughter was not merely sitting at home awaiting their success in marriage arrangements.

Another writer has observed that young Indian women lack interest in the subjects they study (Ross, 1969). In this they differ little from many Indian men. Fields of study are ranked in prestige, and getting into the best profession for which one can qualify takes precedence over the young person's own interests. Thus, as Shils (1961 : 25-26), has shown many Indian intellectuals are in fields that were chosen *for* them rather than *by* them. Part of the lack of interest in education may be attributed to out-moded teaching methods and an emphasis on examinations. Even so, college attendance is so positive an experience in other ways that many young women hope to continue. It provides the opportunity for a free-dom of movement that they have not had before and are not likely to ex-perience again, unless they become employed. Less than 30 per cent of the sample expected to end their education with a bachelor's degree.

Intermeshing of education, employment and marriage system : implications for change

The meshing of the marriage system with education and employment creates potentials for change. A college degree is viewed as an asset in the marriage market more often than is employment. However, under the arranged marriage system, the more education a woman receives the more highly educated a husband she will require. For this kind of husband, the cost of dowry frequently becomes prohibitive. If a woman has acquired her first degree, and a mate is not found, a face-saving alternative is to permit her to continue her education. Her requirements for a husband become even more difficult to meet and her own assets may be declining. Perhaps in anticipation of the possibility that they may have been educated out of the marriage market, many of the respondents maintain that a woman can be happy without marriage. They point to the other alternatives she now has which will keep her occupied. Living arrangements continue to be difficult for unmarried women. Those who see no satisfactory alternative to marriage point to the fact that after her parents' death, the spinster will have to live with a brother and sister-in-law. This is, perhaps, one of the assumptions that Western women will find most difficult to understand.

By many accounts, the practice of dowry is still widespread, and even increasing. The highly educated man has a wider field of potential brides than does his female counterpart. His income is likely to be good and hence he has less need for a working wife. A development which was not anticipated, but which has been noted by several observers, is that caste endogamy weakens when in conflict with the norm that the male be at least as equally educated as the female. Some highly educated women are choosing their own partners, especially when the pool of highly educated men in their own caste is limited. And once these departures take place, the practice of dowry tends to be eliminated or minimized also.

A decadinal contrast

In 1967 it was already apparent that the rising cost of living, of educating many children, and of providing dowry was counterbalancing traditional pressures against keeping women protected within the home. Some women still felt that employment might prove a hindrance in finding a mate. Others recognized the possibility of helping their future husbands financially and also the influence that an employed woman might have in mate selection. Their role might be limited to greater veto power over the parents' choice; however, a small number anticipated that an employed woman could select her own mate. We suggested that some families might begin to weigh a prospective bride's earning capacity against their need for dowry. This still seems reasonable, although, in the short run, there is not much evidence that it has occurred. By 1977, many respondents noted the increased acceptance of working women and considered it normal that highly educated women would seek jobs.

At the time of the original study, only a few types of jobs were considered "suitable" for educated middle class women. Sample members were employed only as lecturers, teachers, clerks and doctors. Teaching has been a "woman's profession" in many countries. Even where female seclusion is a norm, female professionals are required for their education and health care. Medicine, but not nursing, was an early career aspiration for a number of our respondents but only two achieved this aim. Asked about the jobs they would prefer, the women favored that of college lecturer, bank clerk or research worker. In 1977, out of 14 working members of the follow-up group, three were lecturers, one a bank officer, and another a research scientist. In 1967, women who worked gave much of their salaries to their families. This economic role, while new, fits in with more traditional expectations that daughters will be of service to the family and that incomes will be pooled. In the follow-up, most women were continuing to contribute most of their salaries to the household.

The employment problems found most pressing by our sample of educated women, in 1967, were the following : the lack of available jobs suited to their educational attainments, the role of factors such as influence, the need for special kinds of degrees or skills, and the relatively high level of unemployment, even for college graduates. Their concerns focused on the problems of the educated in general, rather than those of their own sex. But underlying many remarks was the assumption that restrictions on the movement of women, and the convenience of working place and time, are important considerations. The working woman may not be permitted to take up residence away from the parental home and, if she does, her living conditions must be carefully arranged. Because of economic necessity, the woman worker is allowed to travel to and from her job, but she continues to be restricted in her social life. While many employed women continue to rely on male relatives for chaperonage on their days off, the accompaniment of female friends and relatives was beginning to be an acceptable substitute. The practice of "dating" was certainly not condoned in Bangalore, although it sometimes occurred surreptitiously. Certainly it would be helpful to examine the social life of unmarried females in such cities as Bombay or New Delhi in order to anticipate trends toward possible breakdown of the restrictions observed.

Problems of educated women

In 1977, restrictions seemed to have lessened. Some respondents wrote that a woman who was working out of economic necessity, and contributing to the family income, tends to have more freedom. And yet another told of a suspicious husband who questioned her about her relationships with men at work. Two-thirds of those responding felt that educated women had about enough freedom to do as they would like, 28 per cent that they did not have enough freedom, and the remainder that they had too much freedom. Respondents still pointed to the difficulty of finding jobs commensurate with one's education, and to the general problem of unemployment. But new problems, that of combining work and home roles, now appeared. One woman wrote, "As I have to perform many duties at home, I am unable to achieve anything in my work. Being a mother, housewife, and an earner, I find very little time for preparation of my classes." And another, "Educated women are finding it very difficult to work, especially after marriage, as they have no place to leave their kids and have no trusted servants." These statements reflect the issues described in other recent studies of Indian working women.

Respondents in the original study considered education to be helpful in making marital adjustments. Most women believed that their broader experiences would make them more tolerant in relating to in-laws, rather than too independent. Those who were already married explicitly described their attempts to cater to less-educated in-laws, in order to show that their education had not "spoiled" them. Of the 19 married respondents in 1967, 68 per cent were living in simple nuclear units. However, of the 24 married women in the follow-up, only 43 per cent were living in such units. This was true although many were living outside of Bangalore, in most cases the location being determined by the husband's work station. In some of these situations, their husbands headed the family unit, but other relatives had come to stay with them. Several women who were living in joint families wrote of the difficulty in having to account for their behavior to less-educated family members, of the compromises they had to make, and the restrictions placed on them. Whereas, in the first study, such women had talked about the importance of adjusting to the husband's family, they now wrote of their own frustrations in doing so. In contrast, one respondent (who herself was living in simple nuclear unit) complained that educated women had too much freedom and that joint families were breaking up because of their independent attitude.

It was anticipated that, as their economic role was recognized, some working women would be freed, voluntarily or involuntarily, from the requirement that they marry. We encountered nine women in the original group who insisted that they neither wished nor intended to marry, this being in addition to one who had chosen to become a nun. Of the five women (16 per cent) in the follow-up group still unmarried, one was the nun and another an engaged woman. In at least one case, the single woman had an important career and a special role in her family, which included other sisters. We saw a woman's professed disinclination for marriage as a way of freeing parents from the obligations of mate selection and dowry. For others, it might be a protest against the arranged marriage system. Most respondents expected their parents to choose husbands for them and to be given a chance to approve the choice. They hoped to avoid any open conflicts with their families, or actions that might hurt their parents. None saw any alternative for the unmarried female but to accept the practice of chaperonage and the need to eventually live with brothers. They recognized the marriage state and motherhood as the prime status through which women gain recognition—and where in the world is it otherwise ? At the same time their desire to work is partially prompted by the wish to be "independent," to have some income and individuality of their own. Here are some comments made by our original group of respondents, which point to dissatisfactions and needed changes :

> The educated girl knows how to behave but she has some independence of mind. She doesn't have to be a doormat. She can think for herself and doesn't have to agree to everything. [A Christian.]

> The trouble is that many [girls] will get their education and then stay at home. There is still the feeling that work is below their dignity. I don't feel that way. They think they won't get good husbands if they work. Women still have that sense of subordination to men. They feel it is their duty. They sit at home and wait to be married. . . In five or ten years all will be working. Because financial difficulties are such now. It is very hard for everyone. The boys even now want their wives to

be earning.   [A non-Brahmin Hindu.]

If you ask many girls whether they prefer to live or die, they will say die.   They feel there is nothing for them, the government hasn't provided.   We feel it would be better to be upper class or lower class.   The middle class girls can't move as freely.   If a girl is lower class, no one will say anything if she goes out to work.   An upper class girl also can do what she wants.   But it is hardest in the middle class.   People will always use their tongues and criticize.   There are many restrictions. [A non-Brahmin Hindu.]

I have a friend whom I want to marry.   He is doing an M.Sc.   In fact, he's doing it because I'm doing my M.A.   My mother is against it. . . He's sort of from a lower caste.   My mother considers ours to be a "big family", better than others.   We're Christians, but from a high caste group.   This boy's aunt once worked as a servant, so Mommy says they're from a lower group.   And he's a little dark.   Mother's always worrying about color.   She'll tell us to put a little powder on when we go out. . . I went to the movies with him last week and I told her, and there was quite a lot of trouble about it.   She calls me a slut and says I am ruining things for my sister.   [A Christian.]

I think the highly educated woman in India still isn't treated right.   She can't do what she would like to do.   Opportunities are limited so she must take what is offered, not what she likes.   Even when she is employed, it is not easy.   There may be difficulty with colleagues.   Each has his own ideas and won't adjust to other people's point of view. There is too much of superiority.   The older people won't listen to the views of the younger people.   They won't consider our ideas, what we think.   [A Brahmin]

Proper opportunities must be given to educated women, for employment and for those who are interested in higher studies. . . They say we should only want to serve, but the money is needed, too, these days for the standard of living.   So how can we not care about that too?   Then people ask how much we earn and they say, 'What, so little with an M.A. ?'   [A Moslem.]

The foregoing comments are not typical.   They represent the views of some of the more outspoken women we met—ones who are willing to express dissatisfaction, and who see the need for change.   Education has not brought the kind of opportunities or rights to which they feel entitled. Much of their concern about jobs reflects the general problems of the educated unemployed. The alternative to unemployment is to take a job that is beneath one's qualifications, something which is hard for an Indian to do. Some young women deplore both the continuing social pressures that circumscribe their movements and also the members of their own sex who uncritically accept an image of inferiority and subordination. Education and employment are beginning to be viewed as mechanisms which will lead to greater independence and more equality.

The picture observed is one of gradual change, but of change that was not easily foreseen a few decades ago. It has been suggested that certain traditional beliefs and practices facilitated some of these developments. Women are now engaged in occupations that their parents would have forbidden a few years ago.

These changes carry within them the potential for further ones. As Musgrove (1965 : 130) points out, "New institutions may be accepted because they seem to lend support to existing social values; but their long term effect may be to undermine them. Middle class parents who now see college education as a natural and even necessary attainment for their daughters cannot control all the consequences that follow. One of the most significant of these is the economic independence gained by the educated employed daughter. Although the educated woman still professes concern and respect for the wishes of her parents and future in-laws, she is gradually gaining in status within the family.

Young Indian women as a group have held a very low position in their families and in their society, regardless of the affection with which they may have been regarded. It is not surprising then that they so eagerly embrace the opportunity that college-going provides. They need not be interested in a particular subject in order to enjoy the freedom and fellowship of their peers that they experience away from home. They need not really care for the content of their studies in order to appreciate the enhanced status that a college degree brings. They need not like a particular job in order to derive satisfaction from earning their own money. The new freedoms and opportunities are, however, still combined with old restrictions and with traditional notions about women's dependence on male protection. The educated woman will have views not shared by her mother or mother-in-law; and some of these views are supported by scientific knowledge she has learned at school.

The employed woman acts both in the status of an educated person who can "mix with" men and women of different castes and religions and, at home, as an obedient, subservient and somewhat ignorant female. The possibility of role conflict is growing. Musgrove (1965 : 126) notes that it was middle and upper class British women of the late Victorian and Edwardian England whose status frustrations led to the militant Suffragette movement. While we have not, in this book, attempted a comparative review of the women's movement in various countries, nor its preconditions, it is obvious that the story of Indian women belongs to such a comparative study.

Women who try to meet the traditional role obligations of Indian wife and mother and also spend many hours away from home in paid employment are experiencing a "role overload" or a "double day". The formerly secluded woman may, at first, welcome her right to work and the independence she feels it will bring. But the reality of such a combination of roles, especially where modern technology has not arrived to eliminate household drudgery, easily creates strain. The educated working woman, when she takes stock, will begin to question the division of labor in her household—a division of labor which has traditionally included many small services to husbands and in-laws. Her questioning, and the physical impossibility of performing all duties well, may conflict with the ideas of a more traditional mate. Some respondents did, indeed, write of demanding or "non-understanding" husbands. The optimism expressed below was not shared by most of the women. A highly educated working mother, now residing in Bombay, wrote :

> With the cost of living constantly rising, more and more husbands are recognizing the need for women to work, and encourage them to take up jobs. They also share the housework. (This is a great change from the traditional Indian male who never helped with household chores and was the Lord of the house.) This is the case with more than 75% of my friends—although a small minority remain the Lordly Egoistic Indian Male Species of yester-year!

Epilogue

To conclude, our initial research represents a first attempt to study recent women graduates and post-graduates in a personal interview situation. Following up ten years later, we were fortunate in being able to contact by mail a fair proportion of the original respondents. The information derived, although used with caution, enabled us to assess some of our earlier hypotheses. New data, especially on the problems of combining work with home roles, finds support in other recent studies referred to throughout the text. A wealth of personal interview data on urban Indian women has now been compiled by some of the researchers mentioned. The advent of International Women's Year apparently spurred increased interest in research on Indian women. In addition, the Report of the Committee on the Status of Women in India has drawn attention to the great variation in the conditions of women throughout the country, and to needed programs. One of the tasks that still lies before those interested in this subject is to examine the impact, if any, of changes in the lives of educated women on the masses of Indian womanhood. The role of women in economic development is a related subject which is gaining serious scholarly attention in many nations and which, hopefully, will be more extensively explored in the Indian context.

INTERVIEW SCHEDULE
(1966-67)

Sociology Department
Bangalore University

Dear Graduate and Post-Graduate :

May we ask your assistance in this research on the role of the woman graduate and post-graduate in Bangalore? It is being done under the guidance of the Sociology Department, Bangalore University. The questionnaire deals with both opportunities and problems of highly educated women. A sample of women has been selected from a list of graduates and post-graduates, and you are one of those selected.

Please be frank in answering these questions. All information will be kept confidential. It will be used only to obtain a general picture of the opportunities and problems of graduate and post-graduate women. Your signature is not required. But please feel free to add your own comments in answering. Thank you very much for your assistance.

Sincerely yours,

Dr. (Mrs.) Rhoda L. Goldstein
Fulbright Research Scholar
Bangalore University

I. Education

1. Please tick off the institution (s) attended, giving degrees obtained and date of graduation :

	Degree	Date
____Acharya Pathasala	____ ____	____
____Bangalore Medical College	____ ____	____
____Central College	____ ____	____
____Home Science	____ ____	____
____Law College	____ ____	____

	Degree	Date
_____Maharani's College	___ ___	___
_____Malleswaram Education Society	___ ___	___
_____M. E. S. College	___ ___	___
_____Mount Carmel College	___ ___	___
_____National College	___ ___	___
_____Rashtreeya Vidyalaya Teachers College	___ ___	___
_____Vijaya College	___ ___	___

2. Major subjects studied _____

3. What other subjects or field did you consider majoring in? (If another subject was considered, how is it that you did not major in this field?)

II. Present activities

1. Are you at present :

   _____married   _____widowed   _____unmarried   _____separated

   If married :   If unmarried :

   (a) Husband's education :   (a) Are you engaged?
                                           _____yes   _____no
   (b) Husband's occupation :   (b) If engaged, about when do
                                           you expect to be married?
   (c) With regard to living   (c) If engaged, please give
       arrangements are you   future husband's education :
       living :   (d) If engaged, please give
       _____independently   future husband's occupation:
       _____with husband's family
       _____other (explain)

2. Is it the custom to accept dowry in your community?
   _____yes   _____no.   Other (explain) :

3. Are you at present :   (Please tick off answer that applies to you)
   _____doing post-graduate studies?   (Give institution and major subject.)
   _____planning to do further studies?   (Please explain.)
   _____not now planning to do any further studies.

4. Please explain which family members have most strongly influenced decisions about your education.

5. How do the above family members feel about a girl attending a co-educational college?

6. Are you at present :

   _____ employed outside home

   _____ not employed; not seeking employment

   _____ not employed; seeking employment

   _____ not seeking employment; would like to work

7. Suppose your family was very well off and there were no financial difficulties whatsoever, would you :

   _____prefer to work;_____prefer not to work. Please explain why :

8. *If you are now employed*, please indicate how family members feel about your working. *If you Are not now employed*, indicate how family members feel about your seeking employment.

   Father

   _____strongly encourages
   _____mildly encourages
   _____doesn't mind
   _____minds somewhat
   _____prefers I stay home
   _____other (specify) :

   Mother

   _____strongly encourages
   _____mildly encourages
   _____doesn't mind
   _____minds somewhat
   _____prefers I stay home
   _____other (please specify) :

   Brother 1 (eldest)

   _____strongly encourages
   _____mildly encourages
   _____minds somewhat
   _____prefers I stay home
   _____other (specify) :

   Brother 2

   _____strongly encourages
   _____mildly encourages
   _____minds somewhat
   _____prefers I stay home
   _____other (please specify) :

   Brother 3

   _____strongly encourages
   _____mildly encourages
   _____minds somewhat
   _____prefers I stay home
   _____other (specify) :

   Sister (s)

   strongly encourages
   _____mildly encourages
   minds somewhat
   _____prefers I stay home
   _____other (please specify) :

Husband/husband-to-be

____strongly encourages
____mildly encourages
____doesn't mind
____minds somewhat
____prefers I stay home
____other (please specify) :

Describe feeling of other influential family members not mentioned above :

9. This question deals with activities other than work. Last week, about how many hours did you spend in the following activities? Please fill in the number of hours before each activity :

(a)____studying and attending classes or lectures
(b)____assisting in the household
(c)____visiting with friends at your home or theirs
(d)____reading for enjoyment
(e)____listening to music at home
(f)____engaging in sports
(g)____going to a restaurant, hotel or club
(h)____going to the cinema

(i)____visiting with family members at your home or theirs
(j)____applying for jobs
(k)____applying for schools or scholarships
(l)____engaging in a type of learning at home. (Please specify what) and number of hours :
(m)____Please add any other major activities and time spent.

10. Do you find that you are busy :

____all of the time
____most of the time

____some of the time
____not at all busy

III.   For those now employed

Please answer the questions below if you are now employed.

III.   For those not now employed

Please answer the questions below if you are *not* now employed.

1. Please describe your position and actual work as fully as possible. For example, if you are a teacher, name school and standard taught. Position is :
_____temporary, or permanent.

2. What are your hours of work? From_____ to_____.

3. Your salary?
_____per_____.

4. How long have you held this position?
_____years _____months.

5. Did your education prepare you for your present work?
_____very much so
_____somewhat
_____hardly at all
_____my education was not needed for this job

6. Do you find your work is :
_____very interesting
_____somewhat interesting
_____not at all interesting

7. Do you find your work is :
_____very tiring
_____somewhat tiring
_____not at all tiring

8. What do you like *most* about your present work?

9. What do you like *least* about your present work?

10. In what way are the hours and place of work convenient or inconvenient for you?

1. Have you applied for any jobs? _____yes _____no (If yes, what was the result?)

2. Have you been employed since graduation?
_____yes _____no. (If yes, please describe your last position and actual work.)

3. How long did you remain in this job?
_____under 3 months
_____3-5 months
_____6-12 months
_____more than 1 year

4. What was the reason for leaving the position?

5. What did you like *most* about that job?

6. What did you like *least* about the job?
If you have held more than one job since graduation, please add the same information about the previous job.

11. How much financial assistance are you contributing to your family per month? If married, how much financial assistance are you contributing to your husband's family per month?

12. How much do you keep for personal expenses per month?

13. Did you work at any other position before taking this one?____yes____no
If yes, for how long?
_____years_____months.
If yes, please describe the position and actual work. What was the reason for changing jobs?

14. What other job, if any, would you have preferred to your present position?

15. Which family members have most strongly influenced decisions about your working?

IV. For all graduates and post-graduates

We would like to have your *personal* opinion on problems of the educated woman. Please remember that this information is confidential, so be frank.

1. Judging from the experiences of your friends and yourself, what would you say are the main problems of the woman graduate in Bangalore?

(*a*) With regard to employment.

(b) With regard to the finding of a suitable partner. Do you think that *education* helps or hinders a girl in finding a suitable partner? Please explain. Do you think that *being employed* helps or hinders a girl in finding a suitable partner? Please explain.

(c) Problems in marriage. What do you think are the major adjustments an educated woman will have to make in marriage?

Do you think that education helps or hinders her in making these adjustments?

At about what age do you think a girl should get married?

2. Under what conditions, if any, do you feel that a married woman without children should work outside the home?

3. Under what conditions, if any, should a mother work outside the home?

4. Do you think that a girl who does not marry can lead a happy life or that she cannot? Please explain.

5. Do you feel you are expected to contribute to the society in any special ways because of your education? Please explain.

6. If a friend's younger sister came to you for advice about going to college, what would you say to her?

7. If you could do anything you wanted to in the next two years, what would you choose to do?

V. Statistical data

Please add the following data about yourself; do not sign your name.

_____age   _____caste
_____religion   _____sub-caste
_____father's job   _____no. of brothers
_____fathers's education   Their education :
_____mother's job, if any   _____no. of sisters
_____mother's education   Their education :

Please tick off which of the following family members are now living in the same household as you :

_____mother _____father _____ grandparent (s)_____brother (s)
_____sister (s) _____uncle (s) _____aunt (s) _____cousins (s)
_____mother-in-law _____father-in-law _____brother (s)-in-law
_____sister (s)-in-law

Please tick off approximate houshold income per month :

____ below Rs. 150
____ between 150-299
____ between 300-499
____ between 500-799
____ above Rs. 800

What class do you consider your family to be?

____ upper class
____ upper middle class
____ middle class
____ lower middle class
lower class
____ other (what?)

THANK YOU VERY MUCH FOR YOUR CO-OPERATION. PLEASE ADD ANY ADDITIONAL COMMENTS YOU WISH TO MAKE ABOUT THE PROBLEMS AND OPPORTUNITIES OF EDUCATED WOMEN IN BANGALORE.

NOTES

Chapter 1

1. This point was made in Amarjit Mahajan (1966) and is by now, a truism. See also Kala Rani (1976).

2. Bangalore was the site of Ross', *The Hindu Family in its Urban Setting* (1961) and her *Student Unrest in India* (1969).

3. At the time of the original study all accredited colleges in Bangalore were affiliated with and their students graduated through Bangalore University. The universe included more than five-sixths of all women receiving degrees that year. Graduates and post-graduates were chosen roughly proportionate to the total number of women receiving the various degrees in 1965. Twenty-eight respondents held degrees higher than the simple B.A. or B.Sc. Since the degree partially determines one's occupational field, the manner of selection affects the distribution of respondents found in various occupations. Because a weighted sample was used, the type of degrees held and occupational status of respondents represent the universe.

. Of the original names and addresses selected, four could not be found and were replaced on a random basis. There were no refusals.

5. Interviews were rated according to the degree of cooperation received. Only two respondents were rated quite reticent or uncooperative, and another 13 per cent somewhat reticent. The average degree of cooperation was one in which the respondent willingly agreed to be interviewed at the time we chose, answered all questions, almost always offered us some refreshments, and chatted with us about other things. We rated as exceptionally friendly those who wanted us to return, who prepared elaborate food for us, who promised to visit the author, or who wanted me to meet other family members not present at the time. We rated almost one-third as exceptionally friendly. In one case a Moslem woman and her husband called at my home to deliver her mail questionnaire, which she had received while visiting her parents in Pakistan.

6. Mrs. Leela Dwaraki, then Miss Leelavathi N. was present at 75 per cent of the interviews, the author at 63 per cent. (The initial "N" stands for Nagappa, the name of Leela's father, but it is not customary for her to use the full name.)

7. Rama Mehta (1970) indicates that her in-depth interviews with educated women from various Indian provinces were all conducted in English.

8. In only one-third of the cases did we find the respondent at home and conduct the interview on the first visit. The median number of contacts required was two but sometimes three or more were needed. Persistence is taken seriously in India, and the determined individual tends to be convincing. Thus, a post-card follow up to a mail questionnaire often led to results . Some respondents apologized for the trouble entailed in reaching them.

9. A number of women volunteered out of context that they themselves did not plan to marry, thus taking an active position rather than a fatalistic one.

10. While Cormack feels that individualism will have an impact on the "group-mindedness" of Hindu women, she maintains that the traditional values of interdependence and harmony will persist and condition the development of the individuality of Hindu women (1961*a* : 193). About this one assistant said, "The submissiveness and resignation in Hindu women which the author discusses is merely superficial. Education has taught the woman the ideas of initiative, equality, individualism and competition."

11. According to the report, the number of girls enrolled in undergraduate courses in arts, commerce, and science for every 100 boys increased from 13 to 24 between the years 1950-51 and 1965-66. At the post-graduate level, the increase was even slightly more favorable. Hidden in these statistics is the fact that girls are poorly represented in engineering, medicine, and commerce—the most preferred fields for men.

12. In Karnataka State, only 22 persons per 10,000 were enrolled in higher education in 1960-61.

Chapter 2

1. Matriculate is one who has finished secondary school, tenth standard (grade).
2. The Cantonment refers to the former Civil and Military Station, that part of Bangalore which was under British administration, in contrast to the part which belonged to the princely state. In 1947 the two parts were merged to form the Bangalore Corporation.
3. Seventh standard (grade).
4. Intermediate and Senior Cambridge both consist or consisted of a pre-college 11th year following secondary school.
5. These figures are assumed to represent, roughly, the proportions of females from these religious groups who were graduated from Bangalore University in 1965. A 1961 estimate of the religious population of Bangalore city is as follows : Hindu, 75.5 per cent; Moslem, 15.0 per cent; and Christian, 9.6 per cent (United Nations, 1961 : 56, Table 7.1). Because of the small number of Moslem and Christian respondents, religion is not used as a major variable. However, comparing the 1967 and 1977 samples with regard to religion, we find there is no significant difference. Chi-Square $= 0.477$, d.f. $= 2$.
6. Two women are unpaid religious workers : one, a Catholic nun, and the other, the daughter of a retired Protestant minister.
7. Béteille (1965 : 15) classifies these groups as Brahmins, non-Brahmins and a third group known by the various names of Adi-Dravida, Untouchables, or Harijans. Béteille's "non-Brahmin" group is sometimes classified as Shudras. For example, Basham (1966 : 134) states, "While brahmins and sudras are to be found in nearly all Hindu communities, there are some parts of India, especially in the south of the sub-continent, where ksatriyas and vaisyas are hardly to be found at all." Others object to the term Shudra, as pejorative and inaccurate.

8. These are, of course, the Brahmins, the Kshatriyas, the Vaisyas, and the Sudras. (Slightly different spellings of some of these terms appear in various reputable sources.)

9. See Barnabas and Mehta (1965 : 72-74). In academic admissions, reservation of seats for "backward classes" usually operates within that group of candidates which has attained the minimum prescribed qualifications but does not score high enough to be selected on merit (Barnabas and Mehta, 1965 : 56). Menon (1966 : 368) writes, "It has been estimated . . . that of 140,000 graduates turned out each year only 2 per cent belong to scheduled castes and scheduled tribes."

10. Pimpley and Anand (1965 : 388) found that educated men seemed to prefer as wives women engaged mainly in three occupations, i.e., teachers, lecturers and doctors. They conclude : "This may be because only these three occupations are considered to be reputable occupations for women."

11. Several respondents or their fathers discussed the problems of early retirement ages for government employees. Some fathers who had held responsible positions were unwilling to seek other work not deemed "suitable."

12. The respondent who called herself lower middle class did so in a very deliberate way. The interviewer writes, "At first she said that she belongs to the middle class, but later said that taking into consideration the income and living conditions she would consider her family to belong to the lower middle class." Apparently respondents did not like to designate themselves as "lower" middle class.

13. If we dichotomize both income and class identification into two categories, the relationship between them is significant at the .001 level, the sum of chi-square = 15.60, d.f. = 1. (Income is divided into above and below Rs. 500 per month; the small categories of upper class and lower class, respectively are combined with the two middle categories, upper middle and middle class.) This correlation of income figures with class is meaningful only in the 1966-67 context. In the decade succeeding our first study, consumer prices for urban non-manual employees more than doubled, nation-wide. Bangalore's inflation rate was above the national average for cities. According to Tata Services Limited (1978 : 165), the consumer price index for this group of workers rose from 132 to 277 between the years 1965-66 and 1976-77; the comparable rate for Bangalore was from 133 to 286.

14. Had we been concerned more specifically with determining class, other indices could have been developed; for example, the possession of a telephone, car or motor-scooter. Interior living space is probably a poor index because the presence of married brothers with wives and children tends to overcrowd homes. Emphasis on educating one's children would seem to be another class indicator, but this is complicated by the relationship of caste and religion to educational values.

15. Another author, Rosen (1966 ; 189-190), details the changing economic position of the middle classes in the decade of the 1950's. He estimates that the lower middle class, defined as white-collar employees with incomes below 300 rupees per month, has doubled in numbers between 1951 and 1961. Regarding their rising expectations, he states, ". . . it is possible that there is now a wider gap between the expectations of this larger group and their accomplishments than there was previously,

since many have not received the great opportunities they thought their education opened to them; and this is a source of potential political unrest. This gap would, naturally, be greatest among the educated unemployed".

16. A variety of nomenclatures is used in Indian states to denote the various stages of education. To simplify, such terms as "matriculate" or "intermediate" have been translated into the number of standards (grades) completed, according to the usage of these terms in Bangalore and taking into account modifications in terminology over the years.

17. Figures on current enrollment of girls, as percentage of the corresponding age group, show that 4.8 per cent of girls in Karnataka State are enrolled in grades 9 to 11, while 12.5 per cent are enrolled in grades 6 to 8. (Government of India, 1966 : 126, Table 6.6.)

18. Other studies might investigate the relationship between high educational level and the presence of sisters. Are different roles assigned to various sisters? One respondent attributed her parents' refusal to allow her to study medicine to the fact that she was the only daughter. A contrasting hypothesis, to which our evidence points, is that the presence of educated older siblings of either sex facilitates the education of younger ones.

19. Dichotomizing income levels into those above and below Rs. 500 per month, and number of siblings into above and below 4, chi-square $= 4.73$, d.f. $= 1$ which is significant at the .05 level.

20. See, for example, *Sociological Bulletin* : 1955.

21. By parental family Shah (1974 : 13-14) means, "a unit composed of a man, his wife, and their unmarried children." Parental families may be complete or incomplete.

22. See, for example, Y.W.C.A. OF INDIA, no date given.

Chapter 3

1. See *Towards Equality*. (Government of India, 1974 : 234-235.)

2. It should be recalled that 29 per cent of the sample already held higher degrees when chosen. We shall consider as "less educated" those having only a B.A. or B.Sc. The "highly educated" or holders of higher degrees include those with master's, double bachelor's, medical or law degrees.

3. For Table 9, chi-square $= 6.961$, d.f. $= 2$, the relationship being significant at the .05 level. Dividing the sample differently, by projected educational attainment, we can group those who hold higher degrees with those now studying for them, and contrast them with those who hold only B.A.'s or B.Sc.'s and are not now studying There is no statistically significant relationship between projected educational level and views about the role of education in marital choice. Nor is there a statistically significant relationship in terms of educational aspirations. However, it is interesting to note that all of the eight women who believe education to be a hindrance in getting a mate fall within the group who now have advanced degrees, are pursuing them, or hope to pursue them. Of the 28 women with one degree who do

not expect to study further, none views education as a hindrance.

4. The Sarda Act laid down 18 and 14 as the minimum legal age of marriage for boys and girls, respectively.

5. Early widowhood meant that the child-bride could never remarry and would suffer the indignities of a permanently stigmatized, childless, physically and socially deprived status.

6. Immolation of widows. If the statement below by Margaret Cousins (1947 : 45) seems to stress the importance of women's freedom unduly, then note the one immediately following, which represents official government thinking approximately 25 years later :

> No movement connected with the freedom of India seems more fundamental than the Freedom for Women's movement. Not all the Governments in the world can give India true Swaraj if Indians themselves, men and women, do not remove the chains of out-of-date custom that hold the higher-class Indian women in impoverishment of body, mind and soul.

The Report of the Education Commission (1966 : 135) states :

> The significance of the education of girls cannot be overemphasized. For full development of our human resources, the improvement of homes and for mould- ing the character of children during the most impressionable years of infancy, the education of women is of even greater importance than that of men. As stated earlier, the education of women can assist greatly in reducing the fertility rate. In the modern world, the role of the woman goes much beyond the home and the bringing up of children. She is now adopting a career of her own and sharing equally with men, the responsibility for the development of the society in all its aspects. This is the direction in which we shall have to move. In the struggle for freedom, Indian women fought side by side with men. This equal partner- ship will have to continue in the fight against hunger, poverty, ignorance and ill- health.

7. Official figures on child marriage may be underrepresented according to the Com- mittee on the Status of Women in India (Government of India, 1974 : 82).

8. See, for example, Khati (1965 : 146-163). Margaret Cormack (1961a : 109-112) deals with the lack of sex education or preparation for marriage of Indian girls. One of the assistants was asked to summarize her reactions to this book. On the topic of sex education, she wrote : "I agree with the author when she states that the complete lack of sex education is wrong and harmful. Even to this day no sex education is given to girls at home."

9. One respondent did not answer this question.

10. A few respondents made a point of saying that they did not feel a highly educated bridegroom was obligatory, but theirs was a minority viewpoint. Of course com- promises with this ideal may be made if the man has other outstanding qualifica- tions.

Chapter 4

1. For a thorough review of studies of women, see Promilla Kapur (1971). Kapur's own intensive field research has contributed greatly to this literature. She has personally interviewed hundreds of Indian women and pioneered in developing information on the taboo area of sexual adjustment in marriage. See, for example, her (1973), *Love, Marriage and Sex*.
2. Since then the American women's movement appears to have shifted the focus of many young women to careers and to a more critical assessment of potential male partners.
3. See Kapadia (1966 : 137); Hooja (1968), and Balasubrahmanyan (1966).
4. In his study of marriage among Kerala Christian Indians, Kurian (1961 : 76) found that 44 out of 60 urban men, as contrasted with 59 out of 65 rural men, had accepted dowry at the time of marriage.
5. In describing changes that have taken place in modern China, he states, "Save for religious virtuoso [s], the 'traditional' Chinese society was almost completely devoid of unmarried adults, either male or female, save in those extreme economic straights when a man could not secure a wife. Neither bachelor nor 'old maid' had any place in the society. The new ways changed this. Careers other than marriage were now open to women, and some women chose to follow them rather than to marry. Unmarried women in professional or worker roles are an increasingly common sight in China, and the marriage age of many other women is being postponed until much later in life than would have been possible in 'traditional' China. Some women remain unmarried because they will not accept a marriage arranged by their parents and cannot arrange a suitable one themselves."
6. Women tend to call themselves girls, perpetually. Even though the respondents' own terminology, "girl," was used in the interviews, the term "woman" has been adopted as more appropriate for our own discussion.
7. If we break down education another way, by degree of education already attained, we find no significant difference between the attitudes of the two groups on this question, and very similar percentage distributions.
8. Kapur apparently agrees with this hypothesis. See Kapur (1973).
9. Chi-square = 6.761, d.f. = 2. The relationship is significant at the .05 level.
10. The YWCA of India has done research on, and directed attention to the problems of housing for women students, workers and aged. See *Y.W.C.A. of India* (no date of publication is given, but according to internal evidence, the study was done in the mid-1970's).
11. Aileen D. Ross, related in private conversation.
12. For Table 13, chi-square = 12.609, d.f. = 2, which is significant at the .01 level.
13. Moslems are generally considered to be more conservative than other groups in family matters.
14. This hypothesis is advanced on the basis of several interviews and observations but not systematic study.
15. For Table 15, chi-square = 11.762, d.f. = 2, which is significant at the .01 level.

16. A recent study of women in Chandigarh found that those educated to matriculation and above preferred 20-25 years as the most suitable age of marriage (Singh, 1974 : 241).

17. In one case there was not sufficient data to make this comparison.

Chapter 5

1. See Chap. 1, pages 18, 20.

2. See Government of India (1974 : Chap. 5) and Boserup (1970).

3. Ross did not claim scientific validity for her sample, which was composed of middle and upper class persons selected by her Indian interviewers. The sampling validity of some other Indian studies quoted by Goode may also be questioned, as he makes clear. However, they are all that is available.

4. Field work was carried out between December 1951 and September 1952.

5. Respondents spoke of sisters-in-law who were not college graduates and who were not employed. A study of the employment rates of less well-educated middle class women would be instructive.

6. The figures exclude one woman who is an unpaid religious worker.

7. Seeking employment need not be a very active process. It often consists of submitting one's name to the Government Employment Exchange and awaiting a call. A period of waiting for results usually follows a job interview or examination.

8. Chi-square $= 4.887$, d.f. $= 1$; the relationship is significant at the .05 level.

9. However, dichotomizing income and class of the "stay at homes" and all others, the relationship is not statistically significant in either case.

10. Dividing respondents into those reporting family incomes above and below Rs. 2,000 monthly, chi-square $= .028$, d.f. $= 1$.

11. The interviewer was assured that, even though she is not allowed to study further, the respondent feels "quite happy," since she is obeying her husband and her in-laws. "This she feels is her most important duty," commented the interviewer.

12. Dichotomizing the follow-up group into those who hold only bachelor's degrees and those who hold higher degrees, the trend for employment to be related to education continues. Chi-square $= 2.994$, d.f. $= 1$. The probability of this occurring by chance is .08.

13. In response to another question about whether or not an educated woman should be expected to contribute to society in any special ways, a number of idealistic responses mentioned duty to "my India" or "my less fortunate sisters."

14. Ross (1961) notes the development of this pattern. At first educated women volunteer to aid the family; later they may be expected to do so.

15. The loss of the father by death is seen as a serious blow to his daughter, who must now depend on less interested male relatives either to find a husband or take care of her for the rest of her life.

16. By significant is meant one who exercises the right to enter into family discussions on the topic. Respondents point out, for example, that the younger brothers "would have no opinions." Sisters' views, while often considered less important,

are known and evidently enter into family discussions. Sometimes a sister was characterized as very "strong-willed"; one who presumably made her opinions known somewhat forcefully and held to them. In the few cases where various sisters were said to disagree, their opinion is marked "other."

17. The following is speculative : If a girl has three elder brothers, it is likely that the eldest not only is highest in authority but has a more distant relationship to her than does a brother nearer to her own age. One might expect the youngest brother to be more sympathetic to the woman's own wishes to work. The strange contrast between viewpoints of the eldest and third brother suggests a different interpretation. The brother who wants his sister to remain at home may feel he is being protective. The brother who encourages her to work may be thinking of her economic contribution rather than her own wishes. Dichotomizing brothers' viewpoints between those who prefer the respondent to stay at home, and those who are encouraging or permissive, we find a statistically significant difference between the opinions of brothers one, two and three. Chi-square $= 6.376$, d.f. $= 2$, and the relationship is significant at the .05 level.

18. Here "important" includes mother, father, husband or in-laws. Of the two remaining, one was a young married Brahmin who did not let out the opinion of her in-laws. She described herself as very wealthy and as being interested in doing volunteer work. The other was a single Moslem M.A. whose family would have permitted her to take a teaching position. Willing to accept only college teaching herself, she had ceased looking for such posts after some refusals.

19. This comparison between the employed women and the "stay-at-homes" yields a chi-square of 29.798, d.f. $= 1$. The differences are significant at the .001 level. The only married respondent known to us to disregard the wishes of her parents and in-laws is a teaching assistant living in the United States with her husband and child. She justifies working by saying that her in-laws and parents do not understand conditions in the United States. Her husband approves of her employment.

20. Brothers but not husbands are included in this analysis.

21. The one woman who is separated is included as a working mother.

22. He states (pp. 33-34), "In urban India caste is increasingly being replaced by individual and class relationships . . . Class factors based on the role of an individual in the economy and society interact with caste elements. The caste and class factors both support and oppose each other, but class elements are more important than caste elements in understanding urban society and pressures."

23. Personal communication.

24. Mehta (1975).

Chapter 6

1. See : *International Labour Review* (1968); Boserup (1970).
2. The National Institute of Social Sciences.
3. Hans Nagpaul (1967) considers problematic the fact that in India "social work has always been understood to be synonymous with voluntary service." Respondents

refer to social work in this way. K. V. Sridharan, who was Director of the
National Institute of Social Sciences has mentioned in a private communication
that many of the well-known schools of social work in India were started by
voluntary social workers.

4. A study by the Indian Council for Social Welfare is said to indicate that there were
about 3,153 social work graduates in 1968 and about 6,000 by 1971 (Government
of India, 1974 : 208).

5. See Pandita Ramabai (1976).

6. This small sample of paid female workers may be considered indicative of the
prevailing rates in Bangalore at the time of the study, since salaries for particular
jobs are fairly standardized. The respondent working in the United States as a
teaching assistant is omitted from Table 22 and certain other tables.

7. Dichotomizing income above and below 200 rupees per month, the difference in
salary between teachers and clerks is not statistically significant for this group.
The figures given represent teaching *salaries*. Income may be somewhat underrepresented, as teachers often take private pupils for tutoring ("tuitions") to supplement their incomes. Students doing post-graduate work may also take pupils, and
one clerk indicated that she was doing so.

8. Salary was a rather neutral question to the senior author, but not to our Indian
assistants. They sometimes asked further questions if a reported salary seemed
unusually out of line. Respondents themselves sometimes found it necessary to
explain how their salaries happened to be so low, adding, for example, "this salary
is only temporary as I am expecting an increase soon."

9. At the time of the first study, one rupee was worth about 13.5 cents in American
money at the official exchange rate. A respondent earning the median income,
between 200-249 rupees, would be earning a maximum of 33 American dollars
per month. This equivalent is cited only as a matter of interest, since costs and
standards obviously differ widely between the two countries.

10. The bachelor of law is frequently taken with the notion of qualifying for higher
positions rather than practising law.

11. Research refers to doing research towards the Ph.D.

12. The practice of having hot lunches delivered from home persists even in the cos-
mopolitan city of Bombay, where the massive problem of distributing lunches to
thousands of workers, and later picking up empty lunch containers, has not
proven insoluble. These containers must be picked up, for the prejudice against
carrying things is still strong in the middle class.

13. Much of what has been said about meals applies only to the middle and upper
classes. Perhaps one of the distinctions made between classes in the city is based on
whether or not members have the right to take specific time off for meals. Servants
generally eat well after others have eaten, and drivers may be on duty for hours
without a real break for meals. Some change is taking place, however. Some of the
postgraduates of our acquaintance are permitted to have coffee or a snack at three
or four places in Bangalore. The university had newly refurbished its canteen

(snack shop) and encouraged women students to patronize it—somewhat successfully.

14. As in other societies, medicine appears to be the one profession the prestige of which can compete with the marriage role. While a number of respondents feel that an unmarried physician can lead a happy and worthwhile life, this need not be taken to mean that women physicians are difficult to marry off. The marriage of male and female physicians appears to be a preferred combination, wherein work and home roles can be made to complement each other. Thus, marriage to a male physician can enhance the woman physician's value rather than creating problems of role conflict. In a somewhat different way, a woman who is a university lecturer will have both prestige and a relatively good salary to offer her future mate, and such jobs are eagerly sought.

15. In suggesting the reform of existing scales of teachers' salaries in higher secondary schools, the Education Commission still proposes "advance increments" for teachers with first and second class in B.A./B.Sc. or M.A./M.Sc. (India, Ministry of Education, 1966 : 55). That is, those teachers having first or second class degrees would receive higher salaries than those who have third class. On the other hand, M.A.'s with third class have been known to obtain teaching posts in colleges. Here other influences come to bear—for example, the preference for a Christian teacher by a Christian college.

16. The dearth of typewriters apparent to the western eye is obviously an illusion; typewriters must be in use more widely if this skill is in demand.

17. What is here represented as religious prejudice might be considered a variant of casteism. Being specifically a Moslem is not as important, for some purposes, as being a non-member of a highly influential caste.

18. Sengupta (1960 : 83) maintains that men are usually chosen over women as social workers in government factories, despite the presence of many women workers who would presumably welcome a woman's assistance. The Education Commission Report stresses the need for women teachers (India, Ministry of Education, 1966 : 63-64).

19. Rosen (1966 : 178, Table 21) shows a 28.5 per cent increase in educated unemployed from the early 1950's to 1961, from 200,000 in 1955 to 1,000,000 in 1961.

20. Chi-square = 7.029, d.f. = 1, which is significant at .01.

21. Chi-square = 11.004, d.f. = 1, which is significant at .01.

22. Chi-square = 5.893, d.f. = 1, which is significant at .05.

23. At the exchange rates in Summer 1977, Rs. 1,000 were equivalent to approximately $116.

Chapter 7

1. See, for example, Thomas (1964); Kapadia (1966, Chap. 11) and Altekar (1962).

2. Despite the anti-Brahmin movement in the South, this sample, taken from all women graduates and postgraduates of Bangalore University in 1965, was 53 per

cent Brahmin. The long tradition of education within Brahmin families, and the advantages conferred by early socialization to it, as well as previously privileged position, help to keep this caste overrepresented among successful students.

3. As indicated in Chapter 2, they appear to be quite representative of the original sample in several important respects.

BIBLIOGRAPHY

AGARWALA, B. R. (1963). Review of *The Hindu Family in Its Urban Setting*, by Aileen D. Ross. *Sociological Bulletin* **12** : 75-78.

ALTEKAR, A. S. (1962). *The Position of Women in Hindu Civilization*, 3rd. edition. Delhi : Motilal Banarsidass.

AMERICAN ACADEMY OF POLITICAL and SOCIAL SCIENCE (1968). "Women around the world." *The Annals* **375** (January).

ANAND, KULWANT (1965). Attitudes of Punjab University women students toward marriage and the family. *Indian Journal of Social Work* **26** : 87-90.

ANEJA, NIRMALA (1966). Use of higher education by women. *Social Welfare* **13** (September) 1-3.

ASTHANA, PRATIMA (ed.) (1974). *Women's Movement in India*. New Delhi : Vikas.

BAGAL, JOGESH CHANDRA (1956). *Women's Education in Eastern India : the First Phase*. Calcutta : The World Press Private Limited.

BALASUBRAHMANYAN, VIMAL (1966). Wedding southern style. *Caravan, The* Fortnightly of National Resurgence, **343** (August 15) : 17-18.

BAIG, TARA ALI (1976). *India's Woman Power*. New Delhi : S. Chand and Co.

BANGALORE UNIVERSITY (1965). *Convocation; Monday the 6th December 1965*. Document of Bangalore University, March 12.

BARNABAS, A. P. and MEHTA, SUBHASH C. (1965). *Caste in Changing India*. New Delhi : Indian Institute of Public Administration.

BASHAM, A. L. (1966). Indian society and the legacy of the past. *Australian Journal of Politics and History* **12** : 131-145.

BENDIX, REINHARD (1967). Tradition and modernity reconsidered. *Comparative Studies in Society and History* **9** (April). (Reprint No. 318 published in 1968 by the Institute of Industrial Relations and Institute of International Studies, University of California, Berkeley.)

BESANT, ANNIE (1913). *Wake Up, India : A Plea for Social Reform*. Adyar, Madras : Theosophical Publishing House.

BETEILLE, ANDRE (1965). *Caste, Class and Power*. Berkeley : University of California Press.

BHATNAGAR, I (1964). Spinsters. *Social Welfare* **11** : 19.

BLOOD, ROBERT O., JR. (1967). *Love Match and Arranged Marriage*. Glencoe, N. Y. : The Free Press.

BONDURANT, JOAN (1963). Traditional polity and the dynamics of change in India. *Human Organization* **22** (Spring) : 5-10.

BOSERUP, ESTER (1975). *Woman's Role in Economic Development*. New York : St. Martin's Press. Originally published in 1970 by Allen and Unwin.

BREESE, GERALD (1966). *Urbanization in Newly Developing Societies*. Englewood Cliffs, N. J. : Prentice-Hall.

CHHABRA, RAMI (1977). A feminist viewpoint. *The Indian Express*, Nov. 5.

CORMACK, MARGARET L. (1961a). *The Hindu Woman.* Bombay : Asia Publishing House. (Originally published in 1953 by Teacher's College, Columbia University.)

CORMACK, MARGARET L. (1961). *She Who Rides a Peacock.* Bombay : Asia Publishing House.

COUSINS, MARGARET E. (1947). *Indian Womanhood Today,* rev. ed. Allahabad : Kitabistan.

DANTWALA, M. L. (1973). *Poverty in India. Then and Now, 1870-1970.* New Delhi : Macmillan.

DATTA, K. K. (1965). *Renaissance, Nationalism and Social Changes in Modern India.* Calcutta : Bookland Private Limited.

DEGLER, CARL (1964). Revolution without ideology : the changing place of women in America. In : Robert Jay Lifton (ed.), *The Woman in America,* pp. 192-210. Boston : Beacon Press.

DE SOUZA, Alfred (ed.) (1975). *Women in Contemporary India : Traditional Images and Changing Roles.* New Delhi : Manohar.

DUBE, S. C. (ed.) (1977). *India Since Independence, 1947-72.* New Delhi : Vikas.

DUTT, G. S. (1929). *A Woman in India (Life of Saroj Nalini).* London : Hogarth Press.

ELLIOTT, CAROLYN M. (1977). Theories of development : an assessment. *Signs* **3** (Autumn) : 1-8.

EPSTEIN, T. SCARLETT (1962). *Economic Development and Social Change in South India.* New York : Humanities Press.

_____(1973). *South India : Yesterday, Today and Tomorrow.* New York : Holmes and Meier.

FELTON, MONICA (1966). *A Child Widow's Story.* London : Victor Gollancz.

GADGIL, D. R. (1965). *Women in the Working Force in India.* London : Asia.

GANDHI, M. K. (1942). *Women and Social Injustice.* Ahmedabad : Navajivan Pub. House.

GEDGE, EVELYN C. and MITHAN CHOKSO (eds.) (1976). *Women in Modern India.* Westport, Connecticut : Hyperion Press. (Originally published by D. B. Taraporewala Sons and Co., Bombay.)

GHURYE, G. S. (1969). *Caste and Race in India,* 5th rev. edition. Bombay : Popular Prakashan.

GIELE, JANET ZOLLINGER and AUDREY CHAPMAN SMOCK (1977). *Women : Roles and Statuses in Eight Countries.* New York : John Wiley.

GIST, NOEL P. (1953-54). Mate selection and mass communication in India. *Public Opinion Quarterly* (Winter) : 481-495.

GOODE, WILLIAM J. (1963). *World Revolution and Family Patterns.* London : Free Press of Glencoe, Collier-Macmillan.

GOVERNMENT OF INDIA (1974). *Towards Equality : Report of the Committee on the Status of Women in India.* New Delhi.

GUPTA, GIRI RAJ (ed.) (1971). *Family and Social Change in Modern India.* Durham, North Carolina : Carolina Academic Press.

GUSFIELD, JOSEPH R. (1967). Tradition and modernity : misplaced polarities in the study of social change. *American Journal of Sociology* **72** (January) 351-362.

HATE, CHANDRAKATA A. (1948). *Hindu Woman and Her Future.* Bombay : New Book Co.

The Hindu (1978). The Position of Women in India, January 29.

HOOJA, SWARN (1967). Dowry system among the Hindus in North India : A case study. *Indian Journal of Social Work* **28** (January) : 411-426.

INDIA (REPUBLIC) MINISTRY OF EDUCATION (1966). Report of the Education Commission (1964-66). *Education and National Development* ["Kothari Report"].

INDIA (REPUBLIC) MINISTRY OF INFORMATION AND BROADCASTING, PUBLICATIONS DIVISION (1965). *The Gazeteer of India,* Vol. 1, Country and People.

INDIAN COUNCIL OF SOCIAL SCIENCE RESEARCH (1975). *Status of Women in India : A Synopsis of the Report of the National Committee (1971-74) on the Status of Women.* New Delhi : Allied Publishers.

INTERNATIONAL LABOUR OFFICE, INDIA BRANCH (1963). *Working Women in Changing India.* New Delhi : I. L. O., India Branch.

International Labour Review (1968). Women in the labour force, Volume 77 (March) : 254-272.

ISAACS, HAROLD R. (1964). *India's Ex-Untouchables.* New York : John Day.

JAIN, DEVAKI (ed.) (1975). *Indian Women.* New Delhi : Government of India, Publications Division, Ministry of Information and Broadcasting.

JANEWAY, ELIZABETH (1971). *Man's World, Woman's Place.* New York : William Morrow.

KABIR, HUMAYUN (1955). *Education in New India.* New York : Harper Brothers.

KANNAN, C. T. (1963). *Intercaste and Inter-Community Marriages in India.* Bombay : Allied Publishers.

KAPADIA, K. M. (1957). A perspective necessary for the study of social change in India. *Sociological Bulletin* **6** : 43-60.

_____(1966). *Marriage and Family in India,* 3rd rev. ed. Bombay : Oxford University Press.

KAPUR, PROMILLA (1970). *Marriage and the Working Woman in India.* New Delhi : Vikas.

_____(1973). *Love, Marriage and Sex.* New Delhi : Vikas.

_____(1974). *The Changing Status of the Working Women in India.* New Delhi : Vikas.

KARVE, IRAWATI (1953). *Kinship Organization in India.* Deccan College Monograph Series, II. Poona, India : Deccan College Post-Graduate and Research Institute.

KEER, DHANANJAY (1962). *Dr. Ambedkar : Life and Mission,* 2nd rev. ed. Bombay : Popular Prakashan.

KHATI, A. A (1963). Social change in the caste Hindu family and its possible impact on personality and mental health. *Sociological Bulletin* **12** : 146-163.

KIRKPATRICK, JOANNA (forthcoming). Themes of consciousness among some educated working women of Bangladesh. **In** : Richard L. Park (ed.), *Bengal : the American Connection.* South Asia Series, Michigan State University.

KORSON, J. HENRY (1970). Career constraints among women grraduate students in a developing society : West Pakistan. *Journal of Comparative Family Studies* **1** (Autumn) : 82-100.

KUPPUSWAMY, B. (1975). *Social Change in India.* 2nd ed. New Delhi : Vikas.

KURIAN, GEORGE (1961). *The Indian Family in Transition : A Case Study of Kerala Syrian Christians*, The Hague : Mouton.

KURIAN, GEORGE (1974). *The Family in India : A Regional View.* The Hague : Mouton.

LAMB, BEATRICE PITNEY (1966). *India : A World in Transition*, 2nd rev. ed. New York : Frederick Praeger.

LEVY, MARION J., JR. (1949). *The Family Revolution in Modern China.* Cambridge, Mass., Harvard University Press.

_____(1966). *Modernization and the Structure of Societies : A Setting for International Affairs.* Princeton : Princeton University Press.

LUNDBERG, FERDINAND and FANHAM, MARYNIA F. (1947). *Modern Woman, The Lost Sex.* New York : Harper and Brothers.

MACE, DAVID and MACE, VERA (1959). *Marriage East and West.* Garden City, N. Y. : Doubleday (Dolphin Book).

MAHAJAN, AMARJIT (1966). Women's two roles : a study of role conflict. *Indian Journal of Social Work* **26** (January) : 377-380.

MALONEY, CLARENCE (1974). *Peoples of South Asia.* New York : Holt, Rinehart and Winston.

MANDELBAUM, DAVID G. (1970). *Society in India*, 2 vols. Berkeley : University of California Press.

MASANI, MEHRA (1973). "Women at Work," *The Position of Women in India.* Bombay : Leslie Sawhney Programme of Training for Democracy.

MEHTA, RAMA (1970). *The Western Educated Hindu Woman.* New York : The Asia Pub. Co.

_____(1975). *The Divorced Hindu Woman.* New Delhi : Vikas.

MEHTA, VED (1978). *The New India.* New York : Penguin Books.

MENON, P. M. (1966). Towards equality of opportunity in India. *International Labour Review* **94** (October) : 350-374.

MERNISSI, FATIMA (1975). *Beyond the Veil : Male-Female Dynamics in a Modern Muslim Society.* New York : Schenkman.

MIRZA, SARFARAZ HUSSAIN (1969). *Muslim Women's Role in the Pakistan Movement.* Lahore : Research Society of Pakistan.

MISRA, B. B. (1961). *The Indian Middle Classes : Their Growth in Modern Times.* London : Oxford University Press.

MOORE, WILBERT (1964). Predicting discontinuities in social change. *American Sociological Review* **29** : 331-338.

MUSGROVE, F. (1965). *Youth and the Social Order.* Bloomington : Indiana University Press.

MYRDAL, ALVA and KLEIN, VIOLA (1956). *Women's Two Roles : Home and Work.* London : Routledge and Kegan Paul.

NAGPAUL, HANS (1967). Dilemmas of social work education in India. *Indian Journal of Social Work* **28** (October) : 269-284.

NAIPAUL, V. S. (1978). *India : A Wounded Civilization.* New York : Random House, Vintage. First published in 1976.

NANAVATI, MANILAL B. and VAKIL, C. N. (eds.) (1951). *Group Prejudices in India : A Symposium.* Bombay : Vora and Co.

NANDA, B. R. (ed.) (1976). *Indian Women : From Purdah to Modernity.* New Delhi : Vikas.

NATIONAL COUNCIL OF APPLIED ECONOMIC RESEARCH (1972). *All India Household Survey of Income, Saving and Consumer Expenditure.* New Delhi : National Council.

NAYAR, KULDIP (1977). *The Judgement : Inside Story of the Emergency in India.* New Delhi : Vikas.

OPPENHEIMER, VALERIE KINCADE (1976). *The Female Labor Force in the United States.* Westport, Conn. : Greenwood Press. (Originally published in 1970 by the University of California, Berkeley.)

PANDITA RAMABAI (1976). *The High Caste Hindu Women.* Westport, Conn. : The Hyperion Press. Originally published in 1888.

PAPANEK, HANNA (1964). The woman field worker in a purdah society. *Human Organization* **23** (Summer) 160-163.

_____(1971). Purdah in Pakistan : seclusion and modern occupations for women. *Journal of Marriage and the Family* **33** (August) : 517-530.

PIMPLEY, P. N. and ANAND, K. (1965). Role of occupation in marital alliances. *Indian Journal of Social Work* **25** (January) : 381-388.

RANADI, S. N. and P. RAMACHANDRA (1970). *Women and Employment.* Bombay : Tata Institute of Social Sciences.

RANI, KALA (1976). *Role Conflict in Working Women.* New Delhi : Chetana Publications.

RAO, G. R. S. (1965). Emerging role patterns of women in family. *Indian Journal of Social Work* **26** (October) : 239-242.

ROSEN, GEORGE (1966). *Democracy and Economic Change in India.* Berkeley : University of California Press.

ROSS, AILEEN D. (1961). *The Hindu Family in its Urban Setting.* Toronto : University of Toronto Press.

_____(1969). *Student Unrest in India : A Comparative Approach.* Montreal : McGill-Queen's University Press.

ROY, MANISHA (1972). *Bengali Women.* Chicago : University of Chicago Press.

RUDOLPH, LLOYD I. and RUDOLPH, SUSANNE (1969). *The Modernity of Tradition: Political Development in India.* Chicago : University of Chicago Press.

SENGUPTA, PADMINI (1960). *Women Workers of India.* Bombay : Asia Publishing House.

SHAH, A. M. (1974). *The Household Dimension of the Family in India.* Berkeley : The University of California Press.

SHASTRI, SHANKUNTALA RAO (1959). *Women in the Sacred Laws.* Bombay : Bharatiya Vidya Bhavan.

SHILS, EDWARD (1961). *The Intellectual Between Tradition and Modernity : The Indian Situation.* The Hague : Mouton.

SHRIVEDI, S. (1965). *A Century of Indian Womanhood.* Mysore : Rao and Raghavan.

Signs (1977). Special Issue : Women and National Development, **3** (Autumn).

SINGH, ANDREA MENEFEE (1975). The study of women in India : Some problems in methodology. **In** : Alfred de Souza (ed.), *Women in Contemporary India* : *Traditional Images and Changing Roles.* New Delhi : Manohar.

SINGH, KHUSHWANT (1966). The women of India. *New York Times Magazine*, March 13, p. 24ff.

SINGH, K. P. (1974). Women's age at marriage. *Sociological Bulletin* **23** (September) : 236-244.

SINHA, J. N. (1977). India : a demographic profile. **In** : S. C. Dube (ed.), *India since Independence* : *Social Report on India 1947-1972.* New Delhi : Vikas.

SIMMEL, GEORGE (1950). *The Sociology of George Simmel*, trans. and ed. by Kurt H. Wolff. Glencoe, Ill. : The Free Press.

Social Welfare (1964). Spinsters, **11** (April) : 19.

Sociological Bulletin (1955). Symposium : Caste and Joint Family, **4** (September).

SRINIVAS, M. N. (1942). *Marriage and Family in Mysore.* Bombay : New Book Co.

———— (1966). *Social Change in Modern India.* Berkeley : University of California Press.

————(1977). The changing position of Indian women. *Man* **12** : 221-238.

STEFFES, ROBERT B. (1976). An occupational attainment index for minorities and women. *The Urban League Review* **1** (Fall) : 29-35.

TAMPOC, RIVA (1959). The Women of India. *Contemporary Review* **195** (January) : 23-26.

TATA SERVICES LIMITED, DEPARTMENT OF ECONOMICS AND STATISTICS (1978). *Statistical Outline of India.* Bombay : Bombay House.

THEODORSON, GEORGE A. (1968). Cross-national variations in eagerness to marry. **In** : H. Kent Geiger (ed.), *Comparative Perspectives on Marriage and the Family.* Boston : Little Brown.

THOMAS, P. (1964). *Indian Women Through the Ages.* Bombay : Asia Publishing House.

UNITED NATIONS. DEPARTMENT OF ECONOMIC AND SOCIAL AFFAIRS (1961). *The Mysore Population Study.* A co-operative project of the United Nations and the Government of India, Population Studies no. 34.

VEETEE (1978). Dowry — the scourge of our time (and all time ?). *Eve's Weekly*, May 20-26, p. 13 passim.

VENKATARAYAPPA, K. N. (1957). *Bangalore* : *A Socio-Ecological Study.* Bombay : University of Bombay Publications (sociology series No. 6).

VERMA, MALKA (1960). Socio-economic study of undergraduate girl students. *Indian Journal of Social Work* **21** (December) : 283-286.

WASI, MURIEL (ed.) (1971). *The Educated Woman in Indian Society Today.* The YWCA of India. Bombay : Tata McGraw-Hill Publishing Co. Ltd.

WOODSMALL, RUTH F. (1960). *Women and the New East.* Washington, D. C. : The Middle East Institute.

YOUSSEF, NADIA HAGGAG (1976). *Women and Work in Developing Societies.* Westport, Conn. : Greenwood Press. (Originally published in 1975 by University of California, Berkeley.)

Y.W.C.A. OF INDIA (no date given). *A Place to Live* : *A Study of Housing for Women.* Bombay : Allied Publishers.

INDEX

Altekar, A. S. 42, 44, 59
Anand, K. 154

Balasubrahmanyan, Vimal 157
Bangalore
   city of 5, 12, 153
   female employment in 88-89
   religious population of 153
   University 5, 8
Barnabas, A. B. 154
Basham, A. L. 153
Bésant, Annie 42
Béteille, Andrè 153
Bhatnagar, I. 54, 69
Blood, Robert O. 58
Bondurant, Joan 4
Boserup, Ester 85, 113-115, 158-159

Career
   work as a 95-96, 129-130
   preferences 130
Caste
   as factor in employment 122-123
   Brahmin, education of 161-162
   identification of respondents 17-19
   Scheduled
      preference to 123
      representation among graduates 154
Chaperonage
   norms about 44-45, 68, 137
   practice of 44-45, 137
China, changes in family system of 157
Class
   Backward classes 19, 154
   criteria of 19-23
   middle 21-23, 25, 154-155
   relationship of caste to 159
Class and
   housing 24-25

income 21-23, 154
meal patterns 160-161
occupation 19-21
Clerical work
   as occupation for women 115-117, 126-128
Committee on the Status of Women in India
   Report of 1, 72, 85-86, 89, 112-115, 134
Cormack, Margaret 9-10, 53, 99, 153
Cousins, Margaret 156

Degler, Carl N. 37
Development, economic
   effect on women's work participation 85-86, 115, 134
Discrimination
   caste 123
   religious 123
   sexual 122, 123
Division of labor, sexual 113
Divorce 35, 112
Dowry
   attitudes toward 60, 62
   cost of 60, 78-79
   practice of 59-62, 77-79
   Prohibition Act of 1961 60
Dutt, G. S. 48

Education
   aspirations and achievements 51, 97-98
   child marriage as impediment to 41
   Commission Report (D. S. Kothari Report) 11-12, 89-90, 156
   commitment to 38-39
   comparative, of family members 26-30
   desire for 48-51, 97-98
   government role in 156
   need for 156

of girls, school enrolements 155
of rural women 86
of women and husband's education 30
of women and siblings' education 28-29,
    155
percent enrolled in colleges 13, 153
percent holding college degrees 13,
    sex 156
unexpected consequences of 135
value of 12, 135
women's generational differences 26-27
women's right to 37-38
Education and
    age at marriage 41-44
    attitude change 153
    caste 92
    employment 85-111, 126-128
    family income 24
    fertility 84
    marital adjustment 79-82
    marital chances 40, 52-54, 74-76
    upward mobility 29
Employment of women
    attitudes of families toward 86-87, 91-
        93, 100-106, 125-126
    attitudes of young women toward 87,
        94-97, 117-125
    conditions of 118-122
    differential rates of 85-86, 88
    dignity of 119
    economic reasons for 86-88, 99
    of married women and mothers 1-2,
        84, 95, 103-104, 108-111
    opposition to 86-88, 91
    place of 120-122
    reasons for 25-26, 86, 90, 108-111
    remuneration in 116-117, 126-128, 131-
        132, 160
    role of government in 123-125
    satisfaction in 117-128
    suitability of 86, 113-116, 118-122
    types of jobs held 88-90, 113-116,
        131-137, 160
    women's right to 1-2, 90

Employment of women and
    caste 91-92
    development 85-86, 115
    education 89, 93, 105
    female roles 89
    female seclusion 113, 115
    marital chances 74-78, 107, 161
    mate selection 75-77, 89
Epstein, T. Scarlett 79
Exchange rate
    at time of follow-up study 161
    at time of original study 160

Family
    attitudes of 100-106
    classification of types 30-36
    disagreement within 101-106
    joint 30
    nuclear, prevalence of 33
    planning, as occupation for women
        115
    relationship of siblings in 159
Fatalism 10, 58-59, 98
Fathers, role of 59, 62, 100-102
Field worker, role of 6-10
Finances, handling of in family 99-100
Follow-up study, authors'
    comparison of samples 11
    comparisons of with data of original
        study 17, 23-24, 32-34, 36, 39, 45, 51,
        71-72, 77, 83-84, 85, 91-92, 94, 99,
        107-108, 112, 131-132, 134-139, 153

Gandhi, Mahatma 42
Ghurye, G. S. 18
Glazer, Nona 111-112
Goode, William J. 61, 86-87, 89, 95, 103,
    158
Gossip, role of 46, 69
Government of India
    Committee on the Status of Women in
        India, Report of. See Committee
        on the Status of Women in India
Gusfield, Joseph 4

Hooja, Swarn 157
Household
    classification of types 30-36
    prevalence of different types 33-36
Husbands, attitudes of, toward wives'
    working 102-103

Independence of Indian women 8-10, 45,
    69-70, 96
Independence Movement 42, 133
Indian Council of Social Science
    Research 12
Individuality of Indian women 8-9, 47
Influence, role of 122-123
International Labour Review 159

Janeway, Elizabeth 2

Kannada, language of 7
Kapadia, K. M. 25, 38, 44, 53, 59, 157
Kapur, Promilla 11-12, 112, 157
Karnataka (Mysore State)
    economic problems of 87-88
    female employment in 89
    Mysore Population Study 88
Kerala 73
Khati, A. A. 156
Kothari Report. See Education Commis-
    sion Report
Krishna, Raj 90
Kurian, George 60-61, 73, 157

Lamb, Beatrice Pitney 37-38
Levy, Marion B. 61, 67
Library Science
    as occupation for women 114
Living arrangements
    of employed women 120-121

Mahajan, Amarjit 152
Mandelbaum, David G. 18
Marital choice
    horoscopes used in 59
    In Japan 58-59

patterns of 62, 73-77
women's role in 53-54, 58-59
Marriage
    age at 41-43, 82-84, 156
    arranged 57, 62-65
    as compulsory for women 41, 61, 63,
        65-69
    as sex-centered 43
    child 41-42
    conventions in discussing 58, 62-63
    happiness in 67
    love 46, 62, 65
    resistance to 62, 65
    significance of, for women 38, 65-69
    suitability of individual for 70-71
    traditional pressures for 61
    women's attitudes toward 58-59
Medicine
    as occupation for women 114
Mehta, Rama 9-10, 12, 35, 60, 112, 152
Mehta, Subhash C. 154
Menon, P. M. 154
Misra, B. B. 19
Mothers, role of 100-102
Muddalinganna, V. 5
Musgrove, F. 141-142
Mysore State. See Karnataka

Nagpaul, Hans 159
Nalini, Saroj 48
National Institute of Social Sciences 159
Nursing
    as occupation for women 113

Oppenheimer, Valerie Kincade 95

Papanek, Hanna 7
Personality
    notion of individual nature 47-48, 70
Pimpley, P. N. 154
Purdah. See Seclusion, female.
Putrika 71

Questionnaires
    use of 5-7, 10

Ramabai, Pandita 160
Reforms, legal
  Dowry Prohibition Act of 1961 60
  Prohibition of Child Marriage Act 41
  Sarda Act 42
Research
  methodology employed 5-11
  use of for policy purposes 1
Roles, female
  changes in 3-4
  conflict in 111-112, 138-139, 142
  models 13
  of married women 108-112
  "overload" in 142
  relations with parents 9-10
  traditional 1-3
Rosen, George 19-22, 111, 154, 159, 161
Ross, Aileen B. 30-31, 33, 44, 50, 53, 62,
  64, 72, 87-89, 135, 152, 158
Rudolph, Lloyd L. 4
Rudolph, Susanne 4

Salaries
  of women in various occupations 117,
    160
  patterns of handling 99-100
  variability in 161
Sanskritization 13, 77, 79
Sarda Act
  passage of 42, 156
Sati 42, 156
Seclusion, female 12, 44-45, 85, 113, 115
Sengupta, Padmini 161
Shah, A. M. 30, 31, 33-35, 155
Shastri, Shakuntala Rao 71
Shils, Edward 129, 135
Singh, K. P. 57, 84, 158
Singh, J. N. 61
Social change
  potentials for 135-136, 141
Social control

community sentiment as form of 46
Social work
  as occupation for women 113-114, 160
Spinsterhood
  legitimization of 69-73
  problems of 65-69
Sridharan, K. V. 160
Srinivas, M. N. 6, 13, 47, 85
Steffes, Robert B. 2

Teaching
  as occupation for women, 89-90,
    114-117, 126-128
Theodorson, George A. 72
Thomas, P. 41, 47, 59, 161
Towards Equality. See Committee on the
    Status of Women in India, Report of
Tradition
  of keeping women busy 43-44
  related to modernity 3-4, 135

Unemployment 118-119, 125, 138

Veetee 78-79
Volunteer work 114

Widowhood
  early 42, 156
Women
  duty of 63
  economic role of 77, 86-88, 99
  freedom of 138-139
  problems of educated 138-139
  protection of 44-45, 67-68
  rural, pilot study of 86
  sexual needs of 68
  status of 1-3, 133-134

Youssef, Nadia Haggag 12
Y.W.C.A. of India 157